A Manual of H

G.A. CHANDAVARKAR

Rupa & Co

Contents

❀

Contents

Preface to the Third Edition

❧

In this edition two more chapters have been added, one on 'The Ethical Religion of the Hindus,' and the other on 'The Theism of Indian Saints'. After the publication of the second edition of this booklet, Principal McKenzie issued his volume on 'Hindu Ethics' in the *Heritage of India Series*. As desired by the publishers we have thought it fit to add a note reviewing the book in general terms.

The subject of Hindu Ethics is of profound interest to all the lovers of religion and we trust that the crystal stream flowing through the current of Hinduism meandering through sunny pools, muddy ponds and clear lakes will satiate the spiritual thirst of man and lead him on to the source of 'New Light'. Forces of evil may be terrific but the ethical religion places before us the ideals of Universal Brotherhood and Spiritual Fellowship, the pious hopes of religious reformers and the magnanimous dreams of many mystics. If the ethical teachings embodied in this small volume were to broaden the intellectual horizon of the readers and ring through the world a tune of harmony, the mighty seers of yore of Hindu India might as well share the credit of being the harbingers of the great worldwide movement of spiritual reaction against the evil tendencies of materialism. If spiritualised science holds that the energy manifested in the mineral and the vegetable kingdom moves manwards, the rishis of this land of religions preached that man's cry is Godwards.

असतो मां सद्गमय, तमसो मां ज्योतिर्गमय, मृत्योर्मा अमृतं गमय

'From untruth lead me to truth, from darkness to light, and from mortality to an immortal Life.' This was the cry (*'Excelsior'*) on to God.

तत्सवितुर्वरेण्यं भर्गो देवस्य धीमहि । धियो नः प्रचोदयात्

'We worship Thee, the Source of all Light. Guide *our* intellects in the path of righteousness.' That is the quintessence of the holy *Gayatri,* which echoes and re-echoes through the chants of every Hindu, a prayer which is as sublime as it is soul-elevating. How does it end? Let there be Peace. Peace and Peace. शांतिः शांतिः शांतिः

My sincere thanks are due to the manager of the Oriental Book Agency, Poona, whose assistance has largely facilitated the publication of the book, and also to Mr N.N. Kulkarni, BA (Hon.) of the Bhandarkar Research Institute, Poona, for correcting the proofs. The manager, Everymans Press, Madras, has taken special care in getting this book printed, to whom also my thanks are due.

Govt. Residency G.A. School,
HYDERABAD, DECCAN,
15 September 1925   G.A. CHANDAVARKAR*

---

* G. Anand Chandavarkar is an eminent economist and settled in Washington DC.

Some Extracts from the Opinions

꧅

1. Sir Rabindranath Tagore, LL D. Kt., writes:

   'Your *Manual of Hindu Ethics* is an excellent book . . . very useful for students.'

2. New India, Madras, (edited by Mrs Annie Beasant):

   'The plan of the book is simple and effective. The sacred books of the east are separately considered in a few preliminary remarks and then quotations from each are given, showing their ethical value.'

3. *The Hindustan Review,* Allahabad, (edited by the Hon'ble Mr Sachidananda Sinha, Bar-at-Law)

   'Mr G. A Chandavarkar, a valued contributor to the Hindustan Review, has reprinted from periodicals a series of papers under the title *A Manual of Hindu Ethics*. It is to our knowledge the first book of its kind and is withal put together in an interesting way. The salient features of Hindu ethics are strikingly brought into relief and the student will find it a safe and instructive guide to the subject We have nothing but admiration for Mr Chandavarkar's *Manual of Hindu Ethics.*'

4. Dr Radha Kumuda Mukerji MA, Ph.D, PRS, Professor, Mysore University, writes:

'I have much pleasure in recommending Mr G.A. Chandavarkar's book entitled, *A Manual of Hindu Ethics* to the notice of all those who have got to tackle the puzzling problem as to how moral and religious instruction can be imparted best to our boys. Mr Chandavarkar has shown a rare discrimination in selecting out of the vast mass of Sanskrit literature some of those texts which convey moral teachings of universal application irrespective of caste or creed and as such are preeminently fit to be inculcated into the young and tender mind. To the Hindus the book must prove to be of special value because it will make the young student familiar with some of the classical passages of Sanskrit literature bearing on moral principles which should be in the mouth of every Hindu boy worthy of the great religion to which he belongs.'

5. Indian Review, Madras: (December 1925)

'It is usually considered that sound moral and religious instruction cannot be given on general lines to Hindu pupils with their diversity of castes and creeds and conflicting doctrines. This manual of Mr Chandavarkar gives the lie direct to such a statement. It is a careful compilation of moral and religious truths from the leading Hindu books . . . preceded by informing introductions . . . The plan is excellent, the extracts suitable and inspiring. The book deserves to be made a moral and religious textbook in every Hindu institution.'

6. The Minister of Education, Baroda State, writes:

   '. . . Your book has been recommended for the use of libraries of secondary schools of this State under this office—Memo No. 3446. Dated 2nd February 1910.'

7. Sir John Woodroffe, Judge of H.M.s High Court of Judicature, Calcutta, writes:

   'I have read your book with pleasure. I think it is a useful work.'

8. The Director of Public Instruction, Bombay, has in his office Memo. No. 3870 of 3rd July 1918 approved and sanctioned the use of the publication for the School Libraries in the Presidency.

9. The Mysore University Magazine: (August 1918)

   '. . . The book will be of real service to teachers engaged in moral instruction in Secondary School . . .'

10. The Benares Hindu University Magazine: (June 1918)

    '. . . Owing to the paucity of books in English on the subject of Hindu Ethics, this book is particularly welcome and deserves encouragement.'

Foreword to the Original Edition

❧

When two nations, with different cultures and traditions, are brought together by Providence in the character of the rulers and the ruled, there is either a conflict of civilisations attended with bitter social and political results or an interpenetration of each culture with some vital features of the other and the consequent enrichment of both. If the politically subordinate nation is unable to contribute to the enrichment of the civilisation of the dominant race, it fails to win esteem and must, needs, depend for the grant of free institutions and the rights of citizenship upon the philanthropic-instincts and pity of the dominant race. A nation fed on pity and crumbs, from the tables of philanthropy, sinks further and further down in its own estimation, instead of becoming, day by day, fitter for self-government, and it becomes more and more devoid of national self-respect, less and less self-reliant. It is for this reason that the civilised nations of Europe, who have learnt their lessons from History, are determined to preserve their distinct cultural existence with a view to become equal partners in the comity of nations. This is why Poland resists to its last drop of blood the Prussian and the Russian effort to sweep out of existence its language, history and traditions, why Alsace and Lorraine refuse to submit to Prussian Rule which is equivalent to the forcible Prussianisation of the French people and the brutal imposition upon them of "German Kultur." Among the ancient nations of the world the

Aryans of India hold a unique position. There is probably no nation on earth as this that was in the past, before the beneficent advent of the British, so frequently subjected to ruthless foreign conquest and exploitation and has yet completely preserved its distinct existence as a civilising agency with a clearly-recognised and definitely formulated cultural mission. What is the secret of this wonderful phenomenon in the social and religious history of the human race? The problem is not difficult to solve. The Aryans of India always commenced an intellectual conquest of the ruling race soon after tendering their political submission. The Greeks swept over India. The result was that the Scythians were completely Indianised and many Greek kings formally adopted the religion and culture of the Aryans. Greek Philosophy, too, was profoundly influenced by Indian thought. We read in the "foundations of the Nineteenth Century" by Chamberlain:

> "That Indian thought has exercised an influence of quite a determinative character upon Greek philosophy is now a settled fact; our Hellenists and Philosophers have, it is true, long combated this view with the violent obstinacy of prejudiced scholars; everything was supposed to have organised in Hellsa as *autochthon*—at most the Egyptians and the Semites were allowed to have exercised a moulding influence—whereby philosophy would in truth have little to gain; the more modern Indologists, however, have confirmed the conjectures of the oldest (particularly of that genius Sir William Jones),"

Next came the Mohamedans. Says Chesney in his "Indian Polity"

> "India presents a remarkable contrast to all other countries which have come under Mahomedan rule, in that when as every, where else the whole population was forcibly converted to the faith of the conquerors the conservative

force of Hinduism exerted a passive resistance which was never overcome.

It may be added that under the influence of Hinduism the Mahomedans of India have acquired many caste practices of a quasi Hindu kind which are unknown to the Notaries of Islam elsewhere."

Aryan culture began to stamp itself upon the thought of Islam from the commencement of political contact between the Muslim and the Aryans of India and perhaps even earlier. When Sind was under the actual rule of the Khalif Mansur (AD 753–774) the Brahmasidhanta of Brahmgupt (Sindhind) and his *Khana-Khadyaka* (Askand) were translated into Arabic by Alfazari and Yakub Ibn Tarik with the help of Pandits. Vyāsa or *Bedyas* the great Vedantist, was known in the Islamic world under the name of Bedya, and therefore, Arabian Sufism owes so much to Indian Vedanta. Later on Faizi translated the Gītā into Persian and Darashakoh got the Upanishads translated into the same language. The latter also believed in the Divine origin of the Vedas. The political contact between England and India has been productive of similar results. In spite of Macaulay's puerile statement that the entire Brahminical literature was not more instructive and valuable than the Æsop's Fables, the historical genius of the Aryan race asserted itself. Seeley, in his "Expansion of England" treats of the danger of the Brahmanisation of England. The earlier race of Orientalists like Sir William Jones, Colebroke, Lieutenant Wilford, Jacolliet and Pocock were indeed profoundly influenced by Indian Thought. Goethe goes in raptures over Śakuntala. Indian Philosophy also began to influence Occidental thought at an early stage of this new political relationship between the Occident and the Orient. Dupperon's inaccurate translation of the Upanishads influenced Scopenheur and through him, generations of European thinkers down to Hegel and Bergson. Indian Philosophical literature has a still more brilliant achievement to its credit. It has dealt a powerful blow to the Theory of "Mental and Moral Evolution and Eternal Progress" to which modern thought seems to be so indissolubly wedded and converted. Alfred Russel Wallace, the joint originator of the evolution theory, on page 8 of his "Social Environment and Moral progress," says

> "In the earliest records which have come down to us from the past we find ample indications that general ethical conceptions, the accepted standard of morality, and the conduct resulting from these were in no degree inferior to those which prevail today though in some respects they differed from ours."

In support of this startling proposition which has stirred the World of Evolutionary Thought to its depths, Wallace cites the ethical teachings of the Vedas and the Mahābhārata and in fact one has only to read hymn 46 of book VI of the Atharva Veda and hymns 34, 71, 117 of book X of the Rigveda to be thoroughly convinced of the truth of the view that the Fount of Indian Ethics the Veda, is indeed Eternal and Divine and therefore, the stream that has flown from such a source cannot but be a stream of ambrosia. Mr Chandavarkar's small volume provides the data of Aryan Ethics upon which a system of ancient Ethics can be built up. As such it is bound to enhance the self-respect of the Hindus and the esteem of the ruling race for their progenitors and may, therefore, be regarded as a valuable contribution to the materials for building up the future culture of civilised humanity which will be compounded of the practical knowledge of the modern world and the eternal and ageless wisdom of the ancients.

The Gurukula University
Kangri. Hardwar
11 July, 1915   Acharya Rama Deva*

---

* (Late) Acharya Rama Deva of Gurukul Kangri, Haridwar, was a highly reputed Vedic scholar and Sanskritist.

Foreword to New Edition

In the 19th century, Hindu ethics came under attack by Christian missionaries and in some ways, this was continued by some sociologists. McKenzie's Hindu ethics represents an unfair Christian presentation of Hindu ethics, the writings of Max Weber, and Dumont's *Homo Heirarchicus* are examples of sociological criticism. The writings of Lokmanya Tilak, Annie Besant, Aurobindo and Radhakrishnan have adequately established the essential nature of Hindu ethics for the modern man. They have reformulated the essential principles of Hindu thought, disentangling it from contingent historical modes of expression. This is necessary in any tradition, the history of which spans five thousand years. Despite changing *Yugadharma, Hindudharma* continues unchanged as *Sanatana dharma.*

Dharma has three aspects. It stands for virtue, right action and ideal ends for the will. The first is termed *adhyatma guna* or *sheel,* the second is *sadachar* or *satkarma,* the third is the *purusartha* that follows from *niskama karma* or *upasana.* The cultivation of virtue comes form the purification of the heart and the realisation of the essential unity or sameness of the self in all beings. It is the separatist force of egoism and egoistic desires that sully the original purity of the mind. Thus, non-violence, love or compassion represent the fundamental virtue. Its cultivation is binding on all without limitation. *Ahimsa, Satya,*

Asteya, Brahmacharya and *Aparigraha,* these five are called *sarvabhaumamahavrat,* the universally obligatory vows. Although universally obligatory, these virtues are ideals to be perfected over a long time, maybe many lives.

Right action has been conceived in two principal ways. One way of looking at it is to consider it as an action consequent on scriptural injunction. Another way of looking at it as an action consequent on right motivation, i.e., on motivation free from *raga, dves* and *moha.* In every case, an action is right if it follows a rightly oriented act of the will. If the will is virtuous and free from sinfulness, the action will be right. More practically, action is in accordance with the duties described by one's station or role in life would be right if performed in the right spirit.

An essential aspect of moral life is living in harmony or *samvaya* and acting for universal welfare or *paropkar.* In fact it has been said:

Paropkarah Puny ay Papay Parpeednam ||

Virtue is helping others, sin is exploiting them.

The ultimate end of moral life surpasses morality itself. If action is performed in a disinterested manner, it leads to the purification of the mind, and thus prepares one for the vision of the self.

It will be seen that *dharma* is rooted in the nature of the self, and expresses itself as the universal law of action and reaction. The universe is not the result of blind chance, it is governed by the law of *karma.* Morality has meaning within the universe governed by this law. It has meaning for the self which does not end with death. The immortality of the soul, its freedom of action *(Svantatrya)* and the law of *Karma,* these are the three postulates of any adequate ethical thought. Doubtless, attempts have been made to construct ethics on a materialistic or a naturalistic assumption. But such attempts end up by abolishing ethics, and replacing it by conventions and sentiments.

The present *Manual of Hindu Ethics* was written nearly a century ago and has gone through three editions. It follows a sound method by giving ancient textual references in detail, so that the reader can have a clear idea of what the ancient Hindu scriptures say. The work thereby gains in authenticity and since it keeps the author's interpretations at a minimum level, it is bound to be long-lived. Its critique of McKenzie's book is particularly welcome.

An important question connected with *Dharma* is about its source. How do we acquire knowledge of *Dharma?* What is its *pramana?* The standard answer mentions four *pramanas,* namely *shruti* or revelation, *smriti* or tradition, *sadachar* or exemplary conduct of good people, and one's own conscience *(antaratman* or *antahakaran).* The standing difficulty here has been the contradictions between the different *pramanas.*

Shrutayo Vibhinnah Smritayo Vibhinnah
Naiko Muniryasyamatam Na Bhinnam |
Dharmasya Tatvam Nihitam Guhayam
Mahajano Yen Gatah Sa Panthah ||

The revealed texts are numerous, the traditional texts are also divergent.

No two sages have the same opinion.

The sense *of Dharma* is hidden in the heart.

One should follow the examples of great men.

Hindu social ethics has been the butt of much modern criticism on the score of caste inequality. Inequality by birth has plagued even modern Western society in the form of race and ethnic prejudice, by the critics that western society in ancient times treated slaves as chattel and till the 19th Century Christian Europe had a feudal hierarchical society where the hierarchy was based on birth, and also the violence and exploitation perpetrated by the white races on the non-Christian and non-white races in many continents including their own. Race and colour prejudice are also based on birth and they played a most important part in recent western history. The fact is that social justice is an ideal still to be attained in practice anywhere. At the same time, we must remember that the basis of the original *Varna* system was *guna* and *karma*. We should not confuse the ideal with the defects that have crept into it with practice in course of time. The stream of social reformers has continued in India along with the conservative ideas from ancient times through *Vedic,* epic, Buddhist, Jain and *Bhakti* reformers till it has at last finally succeeded under the leadership of Hindus, like Dayananda and Gandhi. The reform of Hindu social institution in recent times is a part of this old liberal way of thinking. The western ideas have only been a catalytic agent except for their distortion of it.

I am sure that all those who are interested in Hindu ethical thought will gain authentic information from this valuable book by G.A. Chandavarkar, which therefore, deserves to be highly commended.

PROF GOVIND CHANDRA PANDE*

* Prof. Govind Chandra Pande is an internationally-known historian, philosopher and poet. He has been the Vice Chancellor of many universities including Allahabad University and Rajasthan University, Jaipur.

A Biographical Note
G.A. Chandavarkar (1883–1946)

The author, an esteemed educationist of the Hyderabad State, published successively: *A Manual of Hindu Ethics*, which ran into three editions; an anonymous pioneering biography of Dayanand Saraswati (G.A. Nastesan and Co., Madras); and a widely used textbook on *Ethics for High Schools* (1946). The *Manual of Hindu Ethics* won wide critical acclaim and earned him the accolade of being elected as an Honorary Member of the Royal Asiatic Society of London. It was translated into Urdu (*Hindu Aqlaqial*) by Ghulam Rabbani of the Nizam's Educational Service and into Gujarati by Pandit Trivedi of Ahmedabad. He also authored various original articles on philosophy, history and economics, such as Interpreting Shakespeare in Light of Indian Philosophy (*Hindustan Review*), and archive researched papers on the Mahratta Navy (*Indian Review*), the Treaty Rights of the Nizam for Access to Masulipatam Port (*Mysore Economic Journal*). He was fluent in several languages, apart from English, Konkani, Marathi, Kannada, Hindi, Urdu, Persian, Punjabi, and Sanskrit and also well versed in different scripts, Modi (Marathi), Narq, Nastaliq, and Shikasta (Urdu).

An accomplished pedagogue, he, after a stint at Darul-ul-Uloom, the leading Islamic Seminary of Hyderabad, served as the first Indian headmaster of the magnet school in Hyderabad, the

Government Residency School, succeeding William Adolphus. In retirement, he was appointed by invitation as Archivist to Nawab Salar Jung III, and later founded the Women's Tutorial College in Hyderabad, As a teacher, he was remarkably innovative, unafraid of vexatious rules and regulations. Thus he abolished corporal punishment of students, much to the dismay of the British residency officials, who were brought up on the hoary public school traditions well embodied in the legendary Thomas Arnold of Rugby, who considered that flogging was necessary 'and administered with gravity, given the essential inferiority in a boy as compared with a man.' Remarkably, in his teaching he encouraged students to ask questions in the last ten minutes of the period in an age when even eye-level contact with a teacher was regarded as *lese majesty*. Equally, he was strongly sceptical of the mechanical literary education of Macaulay, crafted to produce 'babus' for the service of the Raj. He felt that what India needed was something akin to the Scandinavian folk-schools systems, a harmonious blend of literary, civic and vocational syllabus. He collaborated with Syed Ali Akbar, then Director of Public Instruction in Hyderabad, who authored an interesting study of the Danish School System and its relevance for India long before the Wardha Scheme of Zakir Hussain and the Indian National Congress. He took the bold initiative of inducting Manual Training and Basic Gardening in the school syllabus. Above all, he enjoyed the lasting affection and loyalty of students of all communities. These included names like Bahadur Yar Jung, the founder of the Ittihad-ul-Muslimeen and the Indian States Muslim League; Suri Bhagvantam, a star pupil of Nobel Laureate C.V. Raman; the Indian Olympic footballers Noor Mohamed and Mohamed Jamal; and several members of the Hyderabad Civil Service. He served with distinction on the Board of Studies in Indian languages of the Osmania University and played a lead role in organizing the Hyderabad Teachers Conference.

For him, the point of ethical theory was to guide action in the world, not to elaborate principles for any ideal world. The deed precedes the world. It was not enough to be good in the spirit of G.E. Moore's *Principia Ethica*. The critical corollary of ethics, which transcends scriptural religion, was to do good. His own life typified this sentiment. It was suffused with the spirit of social reform and service. Despite his modest means, he was an active donor and supporter of the Hindu Orphanage in Gowliguda (Hyderabad) and officiated at inter-caste marriages when orthodox Bramhin priests refused to perform the rituals. He was wholly ecumenical, and synthesised the teachings of the Arya Samaj, Bramho Samaj and Theosophy without being formally associated with them. As a close friend of the Baghdadi Jewish rabbi in Hyderabad, Eliahou Abdallah, he absorbed the essence of the Torah, the Talmud and the philosophy of Spinoza and Maimonides, even as he exposed the rabbi to the basics of the Vedas, the Upanishads and the teachings of Ramanuja and Shankarachrya.

What manner of man was Chandavarkar, and what was his life, background and education like? He was born in the sleepy village of Siddhapur in the North Kanara district of Karnataka in a Chitrapur Saraswat Bramhin family but, sadly, lost his father when he was barely a couple of years old but was fortunately brought up by an affectionate childless uncle in his home at Sirsi, North Kanara. He migrated to Hyderabad in 1900 and matriculated as an external student of the Calcutta University before joining the Nizam's College, Hyderabad, where he attracted the attention of the Principle, Henry Sturge, who was much impressed by his tutorial essays and encouraged him to write in the college magazine. Amazingly, thereafter he studied at the noted Sanskrit Academy, the Gurukul Kangri at Hardwar where he honed up his written and spoken Sanskrit before graduating with high honours from the famous DAV College (Dayanand Anglo-Vedic) at Lahore (now in Pakistan). As always, bereft of family means, he worked his way through college on scholarships and earned his keep in vacations as a working guest in a well disposed family of Mohiyal Brahmins (Punjabi Saraswats) in the Salt Range of the Punjab. He taught English to the family's children and shared the varied chores of shopping, cooking and cleaning.

After graduation, he studied privately, while in service, for the M.A. examination of the Calcutta University as an external student under the guidance of the noted educationist, Herambchandra Moitra of the City College, Calcutta, who, impressed by his earnestness and talent, invited him to be his house guest while appearing for the examination. Moitra, a pillar of the Bramho Samaj, and a deep student of Ralph Waldo Emerson, the American philosopher-poet, was struck by the affinity of Emerson's Unitarian philosophy and the tenets of the Bramho Samaj, which had also a formative influence on Chandavarkar. His educational background thus was wondrously variegated, an Oriental Scholar Gypsy like the medieval scholars who rotated between Bologna, Padua, the Sorbonne and Oxford in search of light and learning.

In sum, he typified the 'Siddha Purusha' in his life and work, and exemplified the spirit of Bradley's classical testament 'My Station and its Duties.' This is an offering of not only filial piety but a pupil's tribute to his teacher.

Finally, my grateful thanks to: Sri Trilokinath Chaturvedi for his high-minded and impressively constructive support for this endeavour far beyond the call; to Vinod Dubey for his varied good offices; to Govind Chandra Pande for his keen interest and writing a foreword; Rupa & Co., Delhi for bringing the new edition; and to Deena Khatkhate for the unstinting moral and logistic support.

ANAND CHANDAVARKAR

Introduction

꙳

The ancestors of Hindus being intensely spiritual in nature fixed
their attention on a life beyond death. They regarded the human
soul as an eternal entity coexisting with the Supreme Being. Every
human soul, they held, was required to go the round of births
and rebirths and reap the fruits of its actions. The eternity and
the transmigration of human soul and the law of Karma form
the cardinal doctrines of Hindu philosophy which preaches that,
when a soul comes to be associated with the gross material
body, it is bound to perform certain deeds and in conformity
with laws divine, reap the fruits thereof. The belief is that, if
good deeds are performed, happiness results and if evil deeds
are done, misery falls to the lot of the doer. The human soul
never dies, it can never remain without doing 'actions' and can
never claim exemptions from reaping the fruits of its deeds. It
reaps as it sows. Ever and anon, man struggles and scrambles
to attain happiness and as happiness is the fruit of Karma, he
should necessarily know what is good and what is bad. Every
law-giver and every thinker of ancient India felt, therefore, the
supreme necessity of framing certain rules of conduct and of
presenting the ultimate end to which all the life of a human
being is to be directed. Sanskrit literature, either of the Vedic or
the Puranic periods, bears eloquent testimony to the existence of
ethical ideas of a superior type. In the history of Hindu thought

it is practically impossible for any one to trace out a period of divorce between ethics and religion. A calm and dispassionate study of the Hindu scriptures will convince any one that ultimately religion and ethics are one. Many of the Hindu institutions have their superstructures built on the foundations of the fundamental principles of the science of ethics. The *Panca-Mahc-Yajnas*—the five daily duties the performance of which is obligatory on every Hindu—typify philanthropy. These five *Yajnas* are (1) *Brahma-Yajna*—Worship of God, (2) *Deva-Yajna*—Reverence to men of light and leading, (3) *Pitri-Yajna*—Propitiation of elders by ministering to their wants, (4) *Bhuta-Yajna*—Feeding the cattle and the birds, and (5) *Atithi-Yajna*—Hospitable treatment of deserving guests. The *Yoga-bhyasa,* the practice of which from the standpoint of a Hindu, is essential for Moksha—freedom from the necessity of going along the ever-rolling wheel of births and deaths is based on Ahimsa – 'mercy to all sentient beings'. Lord Buddha, too, glorified the same virtue and preached his religion only to re-establish the reign of righteousness. From the Vedas down to the Puranas hardly is there any Sanskrit work which does not sing the glory of *Niti*—the ethical religion. Even a treatise on medicine, like the *Charaka-Samhita,* pays a tribute to this and says that physical happiness depends on the practice of morality. Sanskrit poetry, as represented in later dramatic literature, too, first preaches and then pleases. Kālidāsa and Bhavabhūti appeal to their readers more as ethicists than as mere versifiers. Valmiki, Vyasa, Canakya and Bhartrihari are undoubtedly great moralists, worthy of being admired by the students of Plato, Aristotle. Confucius and Laotse. The two *Satakas* of Bhartrihari can very favourably be compared with the 'Meditations of Marcus Aurelius', The golden rule of Christian morals, 'Thou shalt love thy neighbour as thyself' is already voiced forth in one of the hymns of the *Yajurveda*. There can, therefore, be no denying the fact that Sanskrit writers attach great significance to ethical laws or to what they call '*Dharma*' which means 'right thought, right word and right deed.' In immortal strains have the bards, the saints, the prophets and the law-givers sung the glory of Dharma. The devotional songs of Chaitanya, Kabira and Tukarama are echoing and re-echoing the noblest sentiments of sublimest piety. The philanthropic activities of many of the modern religious movements in India have the stamp of this Dharmic revival indelibly marked on them. That moral elevation of the masses is an indispensable necessity for all kinds of advancement is an undisputed fact. In the past, ethical elevation it was that preserved the integrity of the Hindu civilisation. It is owing to the moral vitality that the Hindu race, though often conquered politically, maintained its stability. The history of Hinduism, in all the stages of its struggle with the alien systems of thought, presents the curious phenomenon of its moral victory which is mainly the result of the ethical development of its followers. The power of Dharma has always been marvellous. With its rise nations have risen and with its fall they have crumbled to dust. The world is built on moral foundations alone. In the long run, truth and justice triumph and injustice and falsehood perish. When the poet sang धर्म एव हतो हन्ति धर्मो रक्षति रक्षतः– he meant to say 'Kill *Dharma and* you kill yourself: Save Dharma and you save yourself'. Another poet, too, has the following edifying verse:

धनानि भूमौ पशवश्च गोष्ठे भार्या गृहद्वारि जन: शमशाने ।
देहाश्रितायां परलाकमार्गे धर्मानुगो गच्छति जीव एक: ।

'Man, erring man, all your material wealth shall lie scattered on the ground, your cattle and other paraphernalia shall remain behind, your wife shall bid you goodbye at the threshold of your house, your friends cannot accompany you further than the crematorium. The body shall be reduced to ashes. Only the good deeds of yours follow you. Tread, therefore, the path of righteousness.'

These considerations lead us to the irresistible conclusion that Hindu thinkers have been, from time to time, enunciating the postulates of *Niti Sastra*. But unfortunately in the religious history of India a time did come when, owing to social cataclysms and political revolutions, morality reached a low ebb and religion was shorn of its ethical significance and reduced to a mere heap of superstitious beliefs and meaningless ceremonials. The result of this predicament into which religion was forced was that rationalists and agnostics raised a cry that, in the land of religions religion was no longer a living force. A soul of truth there is in this statement. However, with the advance of education in general, the state of affairs may improve.

The study of Hindu ethics is of paramount importance not only to Hindu youths but also to any student of philosophy, to whatever race or creed he may belong. Hindu ethicists have combined in their systems the different ways of discovering what is right and what is wrong: viz., (1) Appeal to recognised authority, and (2) Intuition. This is particularly the case with Manu. (See chapter IV.) In the classification of virtues some writers frequently refer to three *gunas* (1) *Saloa,* (2) *Rajas* and (3) *Tamas*. In an individual or in a society while the *Tamo-guna* is a disruptive element, the *Satva-guna* is a unifying and an ennobling one. The *Bhagavad-Gita* and the *Yogo-Darsana* enunciate the characteristics of these *gunas*. To evolve moral harmony the development of *Satva-guna* is needed.

Some other ethicists have followed another system of classification. Man, in his relations with society, has to deal with various sorts of people. They may be his equals, superiors or inferiors, and to adjust his dealings with all these he should practise some virtues. This idea has led to the following classification—(i) Duty to one's own self (ā) Duty to one's superiors (āi) Duty to one's equals and (iv) Duty to one's inferiors. This classification of altruistic and individualistic virtues is noticeable among writers, like Canakya. Vidura and Bhartrihari. 'Revere your superiors, love your equals, protect and raise your inferiors,' is the sum and substance of their preaching.

Notwithstanding the fact that there are many sublime ethical doctrines in many Sanskrit works, some misconceptions regarding their end and aim seem to exist. Many there are who tenaciouly cling to the notion that Hindu ethics teaches the philosophy of inaction and in these days of tooth-and-nail competition such philosophy of quietism is of no practical utility. But this belief seems to be the outcome of a superficial study of our scriptures. Let such critics bestow some consideration on the following points and if they, then, think dispassionately and impartially we are confident that they would modify these sweeping statements.

i.   The Vedas, the Upanisads, the Vedānta Darśana and pre-eminently the Bhagavad-Gītā are one and all remarkably opposed to this doctrine of inactive life. Our quotations in the body of this booklet will verify this statement. They glorify what is known as '*Karma-Yoga*'—philosophy of action.

ii. The four well-known *asramas*—stages of life into which the life of every Hindu is divided—give the lie direct to such a statement. The first two stages of a *Bramhacari* and a *Grhastha*—a student and a householder—are stages wherein man is required to lead a life of incessant activity and benevolence. Even in the last two stages man is required to do only such acts as would do good to his fellow-men and advance the cause of education and religion. The life of a genuine *Sanyasin* is, according to Manu, one of useful activity alone. A *Sanyasin* cannot be a *bundle of negations*. He is to work for the preservation of dharma in the society.

iii. A religion which inaugurated the system of four *Varnas* could not have presented to its followers an ideal of inaction. The Hindu law-givers believed that for the proper working of the social machinery, there ought to be (1) an intellectually strong class, (2) a physically strong class, (3) a class whose main business was to work for the material prosperity of the country, and (4) a class that would administer to the needs and comforts of the society as a whole by manual labour. This caste-system of the Hindus has been subjected, in season and out of season to a crossfire of criticism and been held up to obloquy and contumelious condemnation. While the unsympathetic opponents hold that caste-system alone has spelled the ruin of India, the ardent advocates zealously preach that it has maintained the solidarity and preserved the culture of the Hindu people. We, however, do not propose to examine here the merits and demerits of the caste-system. We only hold that a religion which gave birth to this *Varna-Asrama*. Dharma could not have possibly meant that its votaries should invariably retire to sylvan solitudes and lead a life of *'inaction'*.

iv. The end and aim of life presented to a Hindu is the acquisition of *Purusartha-catustaya,* a direct incentive to a life of action. The four aims and objects are (i) *Dharma*—discharge of duty, (ii) *Artha*—acquisition of wealth, (iii) *Kama*—legitimate satisfaction of human desires, and (iv) *Moksa*—final emancipation. These objects preach in quite unequivocal terms that man should *act* honestly and strive for happiness. These considerations lead us to the belief that the system of Hindu ethics does not preach the philosophy of quietism. It advocates a life of strenuous exertion. (*vide* 2nd Verse quoted from *Isopnisad*).

It should also be noted that the lofty ethical and spiritual ideals of Hinduism were reflected not only in the literature of the period but also were they, to a large extent, realised by the people in general in their lives. The testimony of intelligent foreigners, like Megasthenes, the Greek ambassador at the Court of the Emperor Candragupta and the impressions of pilgrims like Fa Hian and Hiuen Tsang are eloquent enough to show that the kings, the officers and the people in general tried their level best to put in practice the moral precepts embodied in their religious literature. The administration of Candragupta, the condition of the then people in general, the description of the *Madhyadesa* and of the charitable dispensaries in the town of Pāṭaliputra as given by Fa Hian about 400 AD and last but not least, the vivid sketches by Hiuen Tsang of Indian life as represented at the Court of Harśa (AD 606 to 608) speak volumes in favour of the high ethical development of the period. Hiuen Tsang, speaking of the simplicity and rectitude of the people observes: 'The people are upright and honourable. In money matters they are without craft and in administering justice they are considerate. . . . They are not deceitful or treacherous in their conduct and are faithful to their oaths and promises.'

Such lofty ethical ideals presented by Hindu moralists deserve to be placed before the young Hindu student, who should necessarily be acquainted early in life both with the theoretical and the practical side of Hindu ethics.

The Plan and the Purpose of the Book

The plan of the book is exceedingly simple. From some of the important works on Hindu ethics, selections are given with their free English translation. The sacred books of the East are separately considered in a few preliminary remarks which are followed by some quotations from those books. The passages are only those that have some ethical significance. In the translation we have tried our best to preserve the original sense of the Sanskrit pieces. It is probable, however, that some of the hymns quoted in the first chapter are capable of being translated in different ways and may not satisfy all the canons of Vedic interpretation. We may say, without the least fear of contradiction, the translation is almost literal but here and there we have added some explanatory terms for the sake of lucidity.

The transcendental importance of imparting religious and moral instruction to Hindu youths is recognised by the majority of educational reformers. The fact that there are. tremendous difficulties in the way is also incontrovertible. In non-sectarian institutions this problem seems to baffle solution. Diversity of castes and conflicting doctrines have rendered the problem so complex that educationists have, at times, despaired of achieving any success in this direction. Even with the best of intentions one is driven to exclaim, 'Let alone religion'. But such indifference is likely to prove disastrous in the end. Hindu youths ought to be early familiarised with the principles of their religion and the history of their institutions. For this purpose suitable textbooks are needed. In our opinion, a textbook, which would give the teacher and the taught select passages from the Hindu Scriptures of ethical significance, is a desideratum. With a view to meet this demand the present compilation is offered to the public. We are, however, fully aware of the fact that neither textbooks nor maxim-grinding in a class for ten or fifteen minutes can work out the salvation of Hindu youths. Much depends upon healthier home and school influences. Such books are more or less guides to a teacher of Hindu theology. In conducting religious classes it is always safer to lay greater stress on the ethical side of the Hindu scriptures. As far as ethics is concerned there are no conflicting doctrines. For all creeds, castes and sub-castes the basic principles of morality are the same. As such, a syllabus drawn up on the following lines deserves consideration and a fair trial in all the institutions where Hindu boys receive instructions:–

In the lower classes stories from Hindu Sāstras, illustrative of different virtues should be expounded. The Hindu epics, the Rāmāyaṇa and the Mahābhārata and the Puranas afford ample materials to illustrate the passages selected in this book. The story of king Dilipa, the ancestor of Rama, the life of Hariścandra. the incidents in the lives of Shriyāla and Prahlāda have one and all great moral significance, The incidents in the noble lives of Indian saints and prophets, like Buddha, Caitanya, Kabīra, Nānaka, Rāmadāsa and Tukārāma, of immortal fame are simply unparalleled in their ethical significance. In the higher classes expositions of these scriptural passages may be given.

Such a scheme of studies has certain decided advantages. A Hindu youth will, early in life, begin to breathe in an atmosphere of sublime teachings and noble sentiments and will have the foundations of civic virtues deeply and firmly laid. He will learn the principles of genuine hero-worship, and of real love for the mother-country and his fellow-beings. He will be better qualified to become socially good, morally sound and spiritually great.

Conclusion

We have only to add that the work is by no means original either in its conception or in the method of its presentation. One never knows how much one owes to friends and teachers, be they men or books. We are deeply indebted to both and to acknowledge every point in detail would be as impossible for us as it would be wearisome to the reader. Still it is with a lively sense of gratitude that we offer our heartfelt thanks to the governments of H.E.H. the Nizam of Hyderabad, and H.H. the Maharaja of Mysore for the patronage, which they were pleased to extend by the purchase of some copies of this book and to encourage us in our humble efforts. Rai Saheb. K. Rangarao, the energetic secretary of the Depressed Class Missions, Mangalore also deserves our best thanks for the special efforts he made in pushing the sale of the book and helping us, in every way, to bring out the second edition.

Hyderabad, (Dn.)
1 January 1917

Chapter I

The Ethical Teachings
of the Vedas

⚛️

The four Vedas—The Rig, the Yajus, the Sāma and the Atharva—are the ancient scriptures of the Aryans. Their rational study is of paramount importance not only to the Hindus and other Indo-Germanic races, but to all students of theology and ethics. Among the books that lay claim to be revealed scriptures they are the oldest. Many eminent Sanskrit authors and profound thinkers of ancient India regard the *Samhitas* as eternal infallible and therefore, the final authority, in matters of religion. The Śatapatha and the Taittirīya Brāhmanas, the Chāndogya and the Bṛhadāiraṇyaka Upaniśads, the Mīmānsā of Jaimini, the Vaiśeshika Darśana of Kanāda, the *Smṛtis* of Manu and Bṛhaspati, the Vishnu Purāna, the Mātrkandeya Purāna and the Bhāgavata, all subscribe to this view. The majestic proportions, the symmetrical charms of some of the *Mantras* and the 'decidedly nineteenth-century-like ideas' thereof have bewildered and dismayed great orientalists like Professor Max-Müller and Griffith. With the advance of Vedic research and with the better and more rational methods of interpretation, the magnificent spiritual value and the unrivalled richness of their ethical contents are bound to be brought to light.

Even the advocates of the Theory of Evolutionary Progress in the moral sphere, and of human instincts as well, are bound to acknowledge that the Vedic teachings are, doubtless, grand and inspiring. In these holy scriptures, sublime thoughts suggesting purity of ideas, truthfulness of speech and nobility of action, are embodied. We quote below some Vedic verses in support of the statement we have made above. It should, however, be borne in mind that many of these verses are in the form of prayers to the Almighty and they present an ideal. In the Vedas, God is viewed as the repository of all virtues, as truth, justice, kindness and mercy, and human beings in their prayers are required to think over and over again all these and then conform their actions to their dictates. Mere repetition of verses is not of any consequence. Herein lies the significance of Vedic prayers:

1. May all things regard me as a friend. May I too think of them as friends. May we all view one another with the eye of a friend.

Yaju. 36. 18.

2. Let us all protect one another. Let us eat and dine together. Let us do brave deeds in union. Let us not hate each other.

3. The giver of life places a truth-speaker in the highest place of honour.

Atharv. 11, 4, 11.

4. We have conquered evil and gained virtue. We are then to be free from sin.

Atharv. 16. 6, 1.

5. Whether in heaven or on earth, let truth be my guardian-angel.

Rig. 10. 37, 4.

6. Mighty Lord! Prompt even a miser to practise charity. Let him be kind in disposition.

Rig. 6, 33. 3.

7. Drive away all disease and impure thoughts. Keep far away from us all thoughts of enmity.

Rig. 10, 63, 12.

8. Oh, Giver of light! Direct our energies in the path of righteousness.

Yaj. 5, 36.

9. Let all (quarters) be kindly disposed towards me.

Atharv. 19, 15,6.

10. May I love every one, whether noble or ignoble!

Atharv. 19, 62

11) May God endow me with wisdom.

Yaju. 32. 16.

12. Bless me with that wisdom that was sought after, by all great and good souls.

13. Protect me from evil action! May I be honest!

Yaju. 4, 28.

14. Oh, the Illuminator of all! I am bound to keep the vow of righteousness. Bless me with strength. Let me enter from the regions of darkness into the regions of light, let me abandon untruth and accept truth.

Yaju. 1. 5.

15. Let our ears listen to what is good, let our eyes see what is good. With a healthy and vigorous body let us complete this journey of life.

16. Love one another with that intensity with which a cow loves its calf.

Atharv. II I. 30. 1.

17. Let the son be obedient to his father and mother. Let the wife always speak kind and gentle words to her husband.

Atharv. 3, 30, 2.

18. Let a brother hate not his brother. Let a sister be not unkind to her sister. With good intentions speak to one other.

Atharv. 3, 30. 3.

19. Be intelligent and submissive: be united, friendly and kind, sharing one another's miseries. Speak gently and sweetly to all.

Atharv. 3, 30. 5.

20. Doing good actions alone live for a full hundred years. There can be no better path than this. Let your actions, however, not taint your soul.

Yaju. 40, 2.

21. By force of celibacy have the wise men triumphed over death.

Atharv. 11, 5. 19.

22. Charity is twice blest; it blesseth him that takes and him that gives.

23. First give to a deserving guest, treat him hospitably and then eat for yourself.

Atharv. 9, 6. 35.

24. May we all be happy. May we secure the happiness of all by conforming our actions to the principles of discipline and economy.

Rig. 5, 51. 14.

25. Most Benign Lord! Source of all energy Thou art. Drive away from us all manner of evil, poverty, weakness, folly, disaffection, hatred, ill-will and all sorts of disabilities.

Rig. 4. 11. 6.

26. Lord in order to make men walk along the straight path of *Dharma* and to develop men's faculties harmoniously Thou subjectest the undutiful to discipline. Let us obey Thy Laws and Commandments.

Rig. 1, 51, 9.

27. Thou bringest perverse people to the company of the noble, the holy and the just.

Rig. 1, 132, 4.

28. Do you walk together in the path of duty, do you think of measures peacefully for your welfare, do you unite to

add to your knowledge, do you tread in the footsteps of learned men.

Rig. 8. 49, 2

29. Oh, men! Direct your energies to promote the good of all mankind. Let your relations with all be characterised by love and harmony. Let your hearts beat in unison with all human hearts.

Rig. 8. 49. 4.

30. Do not return a blow by a blow, nor a curse by a curse, neither mean craftiness by base tricks but shower blessings in return for blows and curses.

Rig. 41.8.

31. Let rich men feed the beggars. Wealth follows the course of the wheels of a running car. It comes now to one and then to another.

Rig. 10, 117. 5.

32. The wealth of a miser is good for nothing. Verily I say unto you that it will be the cause of his ruin.

Rig. 10, 117. 6.

33. Thou art, Oh Lord, power, give us strength.
Thou art energy, give us energy.
Thou art splendour, give us splendour.
Thou art righteously indignant, give us that power.
Thou art Light, illumine our minds with it.

Yajurveda.

34. Let there be peace among bright bodies, let there be peace in the mid-ocean, on the earth, in the water, mineral and aerial worlds and, in fact, throughout the vegetable and the animal kingdom.
Let there be peace, peace, peace, everywhere!

Yaju. 56, 17.

These are some of the verses from the Vedas which place before us the ideals of ethics. That the passages from a very ancient chapter of the history of the human race should contain such principles as 'Bless him that curses you, love all, be honest and truthful' is likely to give a very pleasant shock of surprise to those that have been trained to digest important principles of ethics from the systems of Plato, Spinoza or Spencer. In the unfathomed mines of oriental philosophy there seem to lurk grains of solid gold and 'gems of purest ray serene.' A patient, unprejudiced, discriminating study alone may bring genuine gems to light for the benefit of mankind.

The supreme value of the Veda is recognised by eminent scholars like Prof Max Müller and Griffith.

Says Prof Max Müller:

'In the Veda all possible shades of the human mind have found their natural reflection. It is the first word spoken by the Aryan Man. It belongs to the history of the world and to the history of India . . . As long as man continues to take an interest in the history of his race and as long as we collect in libraries and museums the relics of former ages, the first place in that long row of books will belong for ever to the Rig Veda . . . This treasure of ancient religious thought the sages of the Upaniśads inherited from their forefathers . . . they erected on this ancient foundation—the Veda what was at the same time the most sublime philosophy and the most satisfying religion, the *Vedanta*.'

Says Dr Bhandarkar:

'The germ seed of the Universe is God. The germ seed of the *Dharma* is in the Veda. The essence of the Veda, the fountain head of Dharma is *truth (i.e.* equity, love, mercy) and the basis of birth is *Dama* = self control and *dama* leads to *Moksa* = final liberation—This is all the teaching.'

When ancient sages like *Kanada* and *Manu*, and modern scholars like Max Müller and Bhandarkar regard the Vedas as the most ancient and sacred scripture of humanity they are bound to contain 'the germ seed of Dharma.' They lead man from Nature to Nature's God. They are the warp and woof of Hinduism and seem to be the bedrock on which a solid superstructure can be raised.

Chapter I

ॐ

Sanskrit verses in original quoted in Chapter 1.

1. मित्रस्य अहं चक्षुषा सर्वाणि भूतानि समीक्षे ।
2. सहनाववतु सहनौ भुनक्तु सहवीर्यं करवावहै तेजस्विना वर्धातमस्तु मा विद्विषावहै ॥
3. प्राणाहे सत्यवादिनमुत्तमे लोक आदधत् ।
4. अजैष्माद्या नसामाद्या भूमा नागसो वयम् ।
5. सामासत्योक्ति: परिपातु विश्वता द्यावाच ।
6. अदित्यसंतं विदाधणे पूषन् दानाय चोदय ।
7. अपामीवामपविश्वामनाहुतिमापारिति दर्वित्रामघायत: ।
8. अग्नेनयसुपथाराये अस्मान् ।
9. न: सर्वा आशा मम मित्रं भवन्तु ।
10. पिंयं सर्वस्य पश्यत उत शूद्र उत ।
11. मघां मे वरुणो ददातु ।
12. यां मेघां देवगणा: पितरेश्चोपासते तया मामद्य मेधया अग्ने मेधाविनं कुरु ।
13. परिमाग्ने दुश्चरिताद्वाधस्यामसुचरितेभज ।
14. अग्ने व्रतपते व्रतं चरिष्यामि, तच्छकेयं तन्मेराध्यतां इदमहमनृतात् यत्यमुपेमि ।
15. भद्रं कर्णेभि श्रृणुयाम देवा: भद्रं पश्येमाक्षभिर्यजत्रा: स्थिरैरङ्गैस्तुष्टुवांसस्तनुभिर्ब्यशेम देव हितं यदायु: ।
16. अन्योन्यमभिर्हयत वत्यं जातमिवाहया
17. अनव्रत: पितु: पुत्रां मात्रा भवतु समना: । जाया पत्ये मधुवती वाचं वदतु शंतिवाम् ॥

18. मा भ्राता भ्रातरं द्विक्षुन्मा स्वसारमुतस्वसा समयञ्च: स व्रता भूत्वा वाचं वदत भद्रया

19. ज्या यस्वन्तश्चित्तिनोमवियौष्ट संराधयत: मधुराश्वरत अन्यो अन्यश्यै वल्गुवदंत रातसधो चीनान्व: संमन सस्कृणोमि

20. कुर्वन्नेवेह कर्माणि जिजीविषेत् शतँसमा: । एवं त्वयि नान्यथेतोऽस्ति न कर्म लिप्यते नरे

21. ब्रह्मचर्येण तपसा देवा मृत्युमुपाघ्नत

22. प्रियं श्रद्धं दिदा सत:

23. अतिथिर्यच्छेत्रियस्तस्यात् पूर्वो नाश्रीयात्।

24. स्वस्ति मित्रा वरुणा स्वास्ति पथ्ये रेवेति स्वस्ति न इंद्र। श्राग्निश्चस्वस्तिनो अदिते कृधि

25. आरे अस्मदमति मारे अहं आरे विंश्वां दुर्मतिं यन्निपासि दोषा: शिव:सहस: सूनो अग्नेयं आचित्सचसेस्वस्ति

26. अनुव्रता य रंध यन्नपव्रताना भूमिरिद्र:

27. अपव्रजमिंद्र शिक्षण चिद्रतम्

28. संगच्छध्वं संवदध्वम् सं वो मनांसि जानताम्

29. समानो व: आकृति: समाना हृदयानि व:

30. मावोग्रतं माशपतं प्रति वोचे देव यंतम्

31. पणी यादिन्नाधमानाय तब्ध्यान्द्राधीयांसमनुपश्येत पथां ओहि वर्तते रथ व चक्रान्यमन्यमुपतिष्ठतं राय:

32. मोघमन्त्रं विंदो अ प्रचेता: सत्यं व्रवीमि वधइत्स तस्य

33. तेजोसि तेजो मयि धेहि। वीर्यमसि वीर्यं मयि धेहि। बलमसि वलं मयि धेहि। ओजोसि ओजो मयि धेहि। मन्युरसि मन्युं मयि धेहि

34. द्यौ शान्तिरन्तरिक्षँ शान्ति: पृथिवी शान्तिराप: शान्तिरोषधय: शान्ति: ॥ वनस्पतय: शान्तिर्विश्वेदेव: शान्ति: सर्वं शान्ति: शान्ति शान्ति

Chapter II

The Ethical Teachings
of the Upanishads

❦

The *Upanishads* occupy a prominent place in Sanskrit literature and in them is contained the quintessence of Vedic philosophy. To the treasures of metaphysics they are the very keys. From the dawn of civilisation men of reflective temperaments have been endeavouring to solve some momentous questions. How has the universe come into existence? How and by whom is it governed? What is the nature of human soul? What is true happiness? What sort of a life are we to lead here? Granting that there is a supreme, intelligent, controlling Being, what are the relations existing between that guiding force and the human soul? Of what nature is that primordial personality? It fell to the lot of philosophers to raise and answer questions of a similar nature. In India, the Upanishadkaras seem to have directed their energies to tackle these problems. One has only to study the Upanishads to see what suggestive answers have been proposed by the seers of those ages of antiquity. The inquisitive and the cautious reader is slowly but steadily carried on to the regions of bliss. He is made to fly on the wings of imagination and taken on to a place of perpetual sunshine surrounded by an atmosphere of robust optimism, genuine hopes and sublime faith. There, we are told, all doubts and misgivings perish and harmony, peace and happiness of an indescribable nature reign supreme. Even in this age, when material sciences have made so remarkable a progress as to absorb all our interests, we find men even in enlightened Europe studying these Upanishads and finding solace therefrom.

Says Prof Max Müller:

'The Upanisads maintain a place in the literature of the world amongst the most astonishing productions of the human mind in any age and in any country. . . . They are to me like the light of the morning, like the pure air of the mountains, so simple, so true if once understood.'

Observes Schopenhauer:

'From every sentence of the Upanishads, deep, original and sublime thoughts arise and the whole is pervaded by a high and holy and earnest spirit. In the whole world there is no study so beneficial and so elevating as that of the Upanishads. It shall be the solace of my life and the solace of my death.'

Remarks Dr Paul Deussen:

'The system of the Vedanta as founded on the Upanishads equal in rank to Plato and Kant, is one of the most valuable products of the genius of mankind in its search for the eternal truth.'

Naturally, then, the Hindu heart, too, as yet not lost in the labyrinth of things shadowy, feels itself drawn to that study. That Hindu eye not yet dazzled by the rays of materialistic civilisation casts, 'a longing lingering look' on the monuments of Vedic

Civilisation' and feels delighted. Round the Upanishads there is a halo of sublimity all their own.

The term Upanishad has been explained in different ways. Professor Goldstucker following Pānini holds that Upanishad means 'a mysterious science the study of which leads on to the attainment of bliss.'

Professor Max Müller derives it from the root '*Sad*' to sit, to approach, meaning thereby that its knowledge will take us nearer God. Though the number of Upanisads is not exactly determined, these ten are the most important.

(1) Īśa (2) Kena (3) Katha (4) Praśna (5) Mundaka (6) Bṛhadāraṇyaka (7) Taittirīya (8) Śvetāśvatara (9) Chāndogya (10) Māndukya. Some of these form parts of the Vedas; Chāndogya belongs to the Sāma Veda and Māndukya to the Atharva Veda.

The Isopanishad

This is otherwise known as *Vajasaneya Samhitoponishad* and forms part of the Yajurveda. It is the shortest Upanishad.

1. The whole universe is pervaded by the Supreme, Intelligent and Guiding Power . . . Do not hanker after other's wealth or property.
2. Desire to live for a full hundred years by doing good deeds. Only see that the love of actions does not faint you.
3. For him who views all beings as his own soul there can be no illusion or misery. Love all.
4. Truth is hidden from us by the love of wealth. Remove that veil so that we may understand real virtue.
5. Lead us on to the path of righteousness.

The Kenopanishad

6. How is this universe governed? By whom is it regulated? By Him who is the ear of the ears, who is the mind of the minds and the eye of the eyes: Bold men realising Him attain bliss.

7. We do not say we can fully comprehend Him, nor do we say that He is utterly incomprehensible. It would be far better if we thoroughly realise Him. If not, there would be a great loss.

8. Knowledge gives immortality.

9. Wise men understanding His greatness conquer death.

The Kathopanishad

This is one of the most popular of the Upaniśhads. In the opinion of some scholars, it is said to form a part of the Rig-Veda or the Śāma-Veda. There are in it six chapters or *vallies* as they are called. It begins with a legendary story of *Nachiketas* which is an allegory pure and simple. The story can be briefly told thus:

Naciketa is the son of Vājasrava who, in a fit of anger, consigned him to the God of Death. The obedient son approached Yama and patiently waited at his doors without food or drink for three days. Yama being then pleased with his earnestness agreed to grant him three boons. The first boon prayed for by the boy was the removal of his father's misery and the granting him of peace of mind. The second boon was the imparting of the knowledge of that *fire* which enables one to reach the place of perfect bliss. Both these were granted but the third one was the most troublesome. *Naciketa* begged of him to initiate him into the mysteries of the human soul. He asked him whether it really exists after death. Yama declined to answer this question all at once and endeavoured to wean the child from the pursuit of this kind of knowledge. He proposed to Naciketa that he would give him elephants, horses, gold, etc. But the boy refused to accept them saying that they were all transitory and insisted upon having the knowledge of the soul. Yama then enlightened him on the point. This story is told in a very chaste and sublime style and it teaches one to look for things substantial and not to catch the shadow, leaving the substance.

The second *valli* begins with a remarkable Śloka:–

10. There are two paths, one of goodness and the other of pleasure. The first one may be a difficult one to be trodden at the beginning but in the end, it leads on to happiness. The path of sensual pleasures is indeed pleasant at first but it ends in misery. Wise men follow the former.

11. Those, who in reality live in ignorance but think themselves wise and bold, grope in darkness and are like the blind leading the blind.

12. A wise man, realising that the soul is imperishable and only the body is subject to decay does not fall a victim to worldly sorrow.

13. The knowledge of the soul is not to be obtained by irrelevant talk, neither by a display of intelligence nor by the mere study of *Sastras*.

In the third *Valli* a beautiful illustration is given.

14. Understand that the soul is the occupant of a chariot. The body is the chariot, intelligence is the driver and the mind corresponds to reins. The organs are the horses. (If the chariot is to proceed safely take particular care to keep everything in good order). In the next 7 Ślokas the simile is beautifully expanded.

15. Arise, awake, seek the advice of worthy men. The road to progress is beset with thorns. Wise men say that treading on

it is like walking on the edge of a sword. (Be discreet and cautious. Take time by the forelock. Sleep not, work on.)

16. Those courageous, enterprising, and truth-seeking souls only, who realise that one Soul pervades all the beings, attain perfect and permanent happiness, and not others.

17. Happiness falls to the lot of those who lead a pure, celibate life and who honour truth.

(PRASNOPANISHAD)

18. His knowledge cannot be obtained by those who are physically, mentally and morally weak.

19. It can be obtained by truthful behaviour, by leading a highly moral life and by the study of sciences.

(MUNDAKOPANISHAD)

In the *Taittirīya Upanishad*, a preceptor has to give the following piece of excellent advice to his pupils at the end of their course in the Gurukula. This address may, to borrow a modern expression, be termed a typical convocation address in ancient India, an address which is entirely free from verbosity. It is full of common sense and practical wisdom. It is only a short but sweet form of the address.

Having taught his pupil the Vedas in a proper manner the guru thus addresses him:

1. Speak the truth, सत्यं वद .
2. Lead a life of virtue, धर्म चर .
   Discharge your duties satisfactorily.
3. Desist not from study, स्वाध्यायान् मा प्रमद: .
4. Never forsake right deeds, true words and right action, सत्यान्न प्रमदितव्यम् .
5. Never give up the path of righteousness, धर्मान्न प्रमदितव्यम् .
6. Never hesitate to perform such deeds as would lead to your or society's welfare, कुशलान्न प्रमदितव्यम् .

7. Never be proud if fortune were to smile on you, भृत्यै न प्रमदितव्यम् .

8. Never remain without performing such deeds as would render assistance to your parents and wise men, देवपितृकार्याभ्यां न प्रमदितव्यम् .

9. Revere your mother, मातृदेवो भव = May thy mother be thy God.

10. Respect your father, पितृदेवो भव = May thy father be thy God.

11. Honour your teacher, आचार्यदेवो भव = May thy preceptor be thy God.

12. Treat your guests hospitably, अतिथिदेवो भव = May thy guest be thy God.

13. यानि अनवद्यानि कर्माणि तानि त्वया सेवितव्यनि नो इतराणि = Do uncensurable acts and none else.

14. यानि अस्माकं सुचरितानि तानि त्वया सेवितव्यानि नो इतराणि = Those that are good acts to us, they should be performed by thee and none else.

15. श्रद्धया देयम् = Give with faith. अश्रद्धयादेयम् = Give not without faith. श्रिया देयम् = Give in plenty. ह्रिया देयम् = Give with bashfulness. भिया देयम् = Give with fear. संविदा देयम् = Give with sympathy. एष आदेश:। उष उपदेष: = This is the command. This is the teaching

Taittiriya Upanishad

20. He, who stays in the house of a preceptor, studies the Vedas, then enters the stage of a householder and does not neglect his studies, becomes happy.

Chandogyopanishad

21. He who has not given up bad habits, who has no tranquility of mind and who cannot concentrate his mind, cannot obtain the knowledge of God, even by knowledge.

Kathopanishad

22. Every thing rests upon reason.

Aitareya Upanishad

23. Truth alone conquers and not untruth.

MandakoPanishad

All the Upanishads are unanimous in holding the highest kind of knowledge is that of *Brahma*—God—, and, that man can acquire that by a patient and careful study of the S'ASTRAS under competent gurus and by leading a moral life. Great importance is attached to the life of a celibate—*Brahmacarya*. The theism of the Upanishads is of a rationalistic nature but a discussion thereof falls beyond the scope of this booklet. The age of enquiry was foreshadowed by the Upanishads. It prepared the way for ushering in the age of rationalism reflected in the systems of Hindu philosophy. It produced great intellectual giants of the type of Kapila, Kanāda and Gautama whose marvellous feats in the SHAD DARS'ANAS how the high watermark of intellectual and ethical advancement. One of the Upanishads calls God, as 'Dharmavaham and Papanudam'—the establisher of *Dharma* and the destroyer of sin—True, eternal religion has come from God and it consists of the knowledge and practice of such eternal principles as truth, equity, love, forgiveness, mercy and self-control. The Upanishads preach this grand ethical religion.

Chapter II

༄

The Ethical teachings of the Upanishads.

Sanskrit verses:

1. ईशावस्यमिदँ सर्व यत्किंच जगत्यां जगत् ।
   तैन त्यक्तेन मुञ्जीथा मा गृध: कस्यम्विद्धनम् ॥

2. कुर्वन्नेवेह कर्माणि जिजीविषेच्छतँ समा: ।
   एवं त्वयि नान्यथेतोऽस्ति न कर्म लिप्यते नरे ॥

3. यस्मिन्सर्वाणि भूतानि आत्मैवाभूद्विजानत: ।
   तत्र को मोह: क: शोक एकत्वमनुपश्यत: ॥

4. हिरण्मयेन पात्रेण सत्यस्यापिहितं मुखम् ।
   तत्त्वं पूषन् अपावृणु सत्यधर्माय दृष्टये ॥

5. अग्रे नय सुपथा रायेऽस्मान् ।

6. केनेषितं प्रेषितं मन: केन प्राण: प्रथम: प्रेतियुक्त: श्रोतस्य श्रोतं मनसो
   मनो यद्वाचोहवाचं स उ प्राणस्य प्राण: चक्षुष: चक्षु: अति मुच्यधीरा:
   प्रेत्यास्माल्लोकादमृता भवन्ति ॥

7. नाहं मन्ये सुवेदेति नो न वेदति वेद च ।
   यो नस्तद्वेद नो न वेदेति वेद च ।
   इह चेदवेदीदथ सत्यमस्ति न चेदिहावेदीन् महती विनष्टि ।

8. विद्या विन्दते अमृतम् ॥

9. धीरा प्रेत्य अस्माल्लोकादमृता भवन्ति ।

10. श्रेयश्रव मनुष्यमेतस्तौ संपरीत्य विविनक्ति धीर: ।
    श्रेयो हि धीरोऽभिप्रेयसो वृणीते प्रेयो मन्दो योगक्षेमाद्वृणीते ।

11. अविद्यायामन्तरे वर्तमाना: स्वयम् धीरा: पण्डितंमन्यमाना: ।
    देद्रम्यमाणा: परियन्तिमूढा अन्धनैव नीयमानायथान्धा: ॥

12. अशरीरं शरीरेष्वनयस्थेष्वनपस्थितम् ।
    महान्तं विभुमात्मानं मत्वा धीरो न शोचति ॥
13. नायमात्मा प्रवचनेन लभ्य: न मेधया न बहुना श्रुतेन ।
14. आत्मानं रथिनं विद्धि शरीरं रथरमेव च ।
    बुद्धिं तु सारथिं विद्धि मन: प्रग्रहमेव च ॥
    इन्द्रियाणि हयानाहु: विषयांस्तेषु गोचरान् ।
15. उत्तिष्ठत जाग्रत प्राप्य वरात्रिबोधित ।
    क्षुरस्यधारा निशिता दुरत्यया दुर्गेपथ: तत्कवयो वदन्ति ॥
16. एको वशी सर्वभूतान्तरात्मा एकं रूपं बहुधा य: करोति ।
    तमात्मस्थं येऽनुपश्यन्ति धीरा: तेषां सुखं शाश्वतं नेतोषाम् ॥
17. तेषामेव ब्रह्मलोको यषां तपो ब्रह्मचर्यं येषु सत्यं प्रतिष्ठितम् ।
18. नायमात्मा बलहीनेन लभ्य न च प्रमादात् ।
19. सत्येन लभ्य: तपसा ह्येष आत्मा सम्यग्ज्ञानेन ब्रह्मचर्येण ।
20. आचार्यकुलाद्वेदमधीत्य यथाध्यायमधीयानो धार्मिकान्विधदात्मनि ।
    कुटुम्बे शुचौदेशे स्वाध्यायमधीयानो धार्मिकान्विधदात्मनि
    सर्वेन्द्रियाणे संप्रतीष्ठाप्य हि–
    यावदायुषं ब्रह्मलोकमाभेसं पद्यते न च पुनरावर्तते ॥
21. ना विरतो दुश्चरेतान्नाशान्तो ना समाहित: ।
    नाशान्तमानसो वापि प्रज्ञानेनैनमाप्नुयात् ।
22. सर्वं तत् प्रज्ञाने प्रतिष्ठितम् ।
23. सत्यमेव जयते नानृतम ।

Chapter III

The Ethical Teachings of the Shad-Dars'anas
or
The Six Schools of Hindu Philosophy

⚜

The sublime teachings of the Upanishads heralded the birth of DARS'ANIC philosophy. In that rationalistic age the SHAD-DARS'ANAS stand out as the grandest monuments of philosophic inquiry. These DARS'ANAS are six in number. They are (1) The Sāmkhya System of Kapila (2) The Yoga Dars'ana of Patanjali (3) The Nyāya Dars'ana of Gautama (4) The Vais'eshika system of Kanāda. (5) The Purva-Mīmāṅsā of Jaimini and (6) The Uttara-Mīmāṅsā of Vyasa. The marvellous ingenuity of these philosophers, the acuteness of their reasoning faculty and the coldness with which they promulgated their doctrines have won the admiration of many a nineteenth century scholar. 'What I admire in Indian philosophers,' says Prof Max Müller, 'is that they never try to deceive us as to their principles and the consequences of their theories. If they are idealists, even to the verge of nihilism, they say so, and if they hold that the objective world requires a real, though not necessarily a visible or tangible substratum, they are never afraid to speak out. They are *bonafide* idealists or materialists, monists or dualists, theists or atheists, because their reverence for truth is stronger than their reverence for anything else.' A superficial study of these systems of philosophy makes one believe that there are some conflicting doctrines in them. The Vedantist, for example, is supposed to be a fearless idealist and monist, while the Sāmkhya is recognised as an irreconcilable atheist. But, still, there are a few fundamental ideas which are common to all the systems of Indian philosophy. They all perceived that everything material is subject to change and that there is misery all round. The world, they believed, is full of suffering. This idea has led many critics to charge Hindu philosophers with hopeless pessimism. But Prof Max Müller, in his admirable work on '*Six Systems of Indian Philosophy,*' pertinently observes—'Indian philosophers are by no means dwelling for ever on the miseries of life. They are not always whining or protesting that life is not worth living. That is not their pessimism. They simply state that they received their first impulse to philosophic reflection from the fact that there is suffering in the world. They evidently thought that, in a perfect world, suffering had no place, that it is something anomalous, something at all events to be accounted for, and, if possible, to be overcome. Pain, certainly, seems to be an imperfection, and, as such, may well have caused the question why it existed and how it could be annihilated. But this is not the disposition which we are accustomed to call pessimism.' Naturally, then, were all the thoughts of the philosophers directed to trace the origin of evil, pain and sufferings. The next conception which underlies all the systems is that ignorance is the cause of all misery. This ignorance or want of true knowledge is called by different names by different thinkers. The 'AVIVEKA' of Sāmkhya, the 'AVIDYA' of the Vedanta, and the 'MITHYA-JNANA' of Nyāya are all synonyms for their conception of ignorance as the cause of all sufferings. Ultimately they denote and connote only one meaning. For all practical purposes, 'non-discrimination', 'nescience' and 'false knowledge' mean the same thing. Having once established the fact that the root cause of all our sufferings is in our own want of true knowledge, the different systems point out that self-culture alone can lead to salvation. If the paths of this self-culture seem to be different, the goal of all seems to be *one* only. They all believe in the immortality of human soul. This soul is held in bondage of ignorance and its salvation lies in the severance of that bondage. That bondage can be severed by true knowledge alone. The MOKSHA of Hindu philosophy is the ultimate goal. True knowledge can save the soul; VIDYA alone can cut asunder the carnal bonds and make the soul dwell in moral and spiritual grandeur. The soul unlike the flesh is heavenly. Its deep attachment to sensual objects is pernicious and there ought to be the sublime consciousness of a higher and a nobler purpose of life. The NIRVANA of Indian philosophy is the complete freedom of the soul from all limitations. The VEDANTA goes a step further. Its idealism makes the human soul ultimately become one with the Universal Spirit. The YOGA DARS'ANA of Patanjali pre-eminently suggests the path of achieving this freedom from the meshes of matter. A brief analysis of these different systems of thought, based on the ideas presented by Mr P.N. Bose in his remarkable *Epochs of Civilisation*, may not prove uninteresting to many of our readers.

The Sāmkhya System

This is the oldest, the boldest and the most profound of all the systems. Kapila, the author of this system, first seeks to answer the question, 'What is the object of man's strugglings?'

1. अथ त्रिविधदुःखात्सन्तनिवृत्तिरत्यन्तपुरुषार्थः:– The highest and noblest aim of man is to ward off three sorts of evils:–

   1. ADHYATMIK—those proceeding from self, bodily pain and diseases of mind,
   2. ADHI-BHAUTIK—those proceeding from other beings, and
   3. ADHI-DAIVIKA—those proceeding from elements.

   (Ch. I. 1).

2. He holds that human soul is different from body, शरीरादिव्यतिरिक्त: पुमान्

   (Ch. I. 139).

3. Freedem from bondage and beatitude result from true knowledge, ज्ञानान्मुक्ति:

   (Ch. III. 23).

4. When the five organs of senses come in contact with the objects, pleasure or pain results पञ्चावयवयोगात् सुखसंवित्ति:

   (Ch. V. Su. 27)

5. That advice alone is acceptable which is given by the wise, the unprejudiced and the good intentioned and such advice is law, आप्तोपदेश: शब्द:

   (Ch. I, 101).

6. Success to him who is without deep attachment to unreal things of the world, विरक्तस्य तत्सिद्धे:

   (Ch. II, 2).

Kapila starts with denying the efficacy of rites and ceremonials. He would admit nothing that could not be known by the three kinds of evidence recognised by him—perception, inference and testimony. He would not admit the existence of an active Supreme Being as it could not be proved by such evidence, (ईश्वरोऽसिद्धे). 'This atheism,' says Max Müller, 'was very different from what we mean by it. It was the negation of the necessity of admitting an active or limted personal god and hence was carefully distinguished in

India from the atheism of the NASTIKAS—Nihilists—, who denied
the existence of anything transcendent, of anything beyond our
bodily senses, of anything divine.' This philosophy is dualistic.
According to it, there are two fundamental principles of being, the
subject and the object, the ego and the non-ego, the self and the
not-self. The object is PRAKRITI, Nature, the unmanifest, eternal,
primordial principle. Kapila is an uncompromising evolutionist.
The whole world, everything except soul, has been evolved,
according to him, out of this primal agent. The order of evolution
has been from the homogeneous to the heterogeneous, from
the subtle to the gross, from the simple to the complex. The
undifferentiated PRAKRITI is regarded as the equipoised condition
of the three forces—*Satva, Rajas,* and *Tamas*—(1) the force of
stable existence, (2) the force of attraction, and (3) the force of
repulsion. The evolution of the various objects of our experience
from non-differentiated, formless, primary matter is effected by
the intervention of Purusha, Soul, the principle of intelligence.
According to Kapila each soul is separate and leads a separate
existence after its emancipation from the bonds of nescience.
He believes in the transmigration of souls and assumes that
even the subtle body (LINGA S'ARIRA), the *Manas* and the subtle
principles migrate with the soul. When the soul has acquired
discriminative knowledge, and recognises that it is different
from the object-world the chain of migration is snapped and
it stands free. Thenceforth it dwells in beatitude and in blissful
contemplation of its own nature.

The Yoga-Dars'ana

Patanjali is the author of these *Yoga* aphorisms. The book is
divided into four chapters and has nearly two hundred SUTRAS.
In addition to his remarkable work on *Yoga,* he has written a
great commentary on Pāṇini's grammar as well as a work on

medicine. Both as a grammarian and a physican he is eminently fitted to be a writer on philosophy. He seems to administer to man's physical, mental and spiritual needs.

The word 'Yoga' means union and is derived from a´ root, meaning 'to join'. It is a science which teaches one the method of joining the human soul with the Supreme Spirit. The author believes in three eternal coexistent entities, God, Man and the Matter. Man having fallen from a pristine state of purity is involved in matter and this science of Yoga suggests the method of extricating the soul from its meshes. Of the several methods suggested the best and the safest method of Yoga is the *Love of God*. Loving God with all one's heart and soul would quickly bring about the cessation of all mental functions. The following are the moral attributes that an aspirant must try to cultivate: 'He must show happiness and feel happiness when dealing with those who are happy. Let him have no feeling of jealousy towards them. He must show compassion towards those who are suffering. He must not be callous to the miseries of others. He must be complacent towards the virtuous, and hate not the sinner.' (Rai Bahadur S.C. Vasu's Introductions to Patanjali's Yoga Sutras, Pānini Office).

Patanjali is chiefly concerned with the steadying of the mind. Yoga is the restraint, and the suppression of all the actions and the functions of the mind to guide it in one channel of supreme bliss. To attain tranquility of mind there are various obstacles—doubt, lethargy, passionate attachment and wrong perception. These must be removed first, before self-culture can be an accomplished fact. The accessaries of Yoga are eight-fold:

I. YAMA:– Practise restraint—This consists of five sub-divisions—

तत्राहिंसासत्यास्तेयब्रह्मचर्यापरिग्रहा यमा

(Ch. II. 30.)

(a) AHIMSA—abstinence from injury
(b) SATYA—Truthfulness,

(c) ASTYEA—abstinence from theft,

(d) BRAHMACHARYA—Continence,

(e) and, APARIGRAHA—Abstinence from avariciousness.

Vyāsa's commentary on this Sutra is grand. He defines AHIMSA thus:

सर्वथा सर्वथा सर्वभूतानां अनभिद्रोहः :— It consists in not causing pain to any living creature in any way at any time.

Veracity consists in word and thought being in accord with facts. Speech is uttered for the purpose of transferring one's knowledge to others. It should be employed only for the good of others and not for their injury. If the speech proves injurious to living beings it is not truth; it is a sin only. Let every one examine well and then utter truth for the benefit of all living beings. Theft is the making one's own unlawfully of things belonging to others. Abstinence from theft consists in the absence of the desire thereof. Continence is the restraint of the power of generation. Sensations giving rise to incontinence, such as the desire of seeing and speaking to women, are to be checked. Absence of avariciousness is the non-appropriation of things not one's own. Avarice leads to attachment and attachment to the repetition of enjoyment.

II. The following five are the sub-divisions of NIYAMAS—observances—

शोचसन्तोषतपःस्वाध्यायेश्वरप्रणिधानानि नियमाः :— The observences are (1) Purity of mind and body, (2) Contentment, (3) Purificatory action, (4) Study and (5) Making of God the motive of all action. Purity of body can be brought about by water and consists in the eating of pure and wholesome things. Internal purity consists in keeping the mind pure and in weaning it away from evil tendencies and thoughts. Contentment is the absence of mean desire to secure more of the necessaries of life than one already possesses. Purificatory action consists in the endurance of the pairs of opposites, such as heat and cold; study is the acquisition of scientific knowledge and the repetition of the syllable OM. The making of Īs'vara the motive of all actions means the doing of all actions to fulfil the purpose of God.

III. ASANA:– स्थिरसुखमासनम् (II.46). Steady posture of the body. Different postures are described to aid concentration. These are useful as physical excercises also.

IV. PRANAYAMA:– Regular control of breath. Deep breathing maintains physical vigour and helps concentration.

V. PRATYAHARA:– Control of senses. Different organs have different cravings. They must be brought under effective control. It is abstraction.

VI. DHARANA:– Steadiness of mind by confining it to any one object.

VII. DHYANA:– Contemplation of one object to the exclusion of all others.

VIII. SAMADHI:– Profound meditation, or absorption, by which mind is thoroughly collected and remains fixed on one point. These eight accessories are embodied in the following aphorism:–

यमनियमासनप्राणायामप्रत्याहारधारणाध्यनसमाधयोऽष्टाङ्गानि

(Ch. II. 29)

He defines Yoga thus:–

योगश्चित्तेवृत्तिनिरोध:

(Ch. I. 9)

Yoga is the restraint of mental modification. The control of mind can be effected thus:– अभ्यासावैराग्याभ्याम् तन्निरोध:—

(I. 12).

Mind can be restrained by practice and desirelessness. The stream of mind flows both ways, flows towards good and evil. That which flows on to perfect independence down the plane of discriminating knowledge is named the stream of happiness. That which flows down the plane of undiscriminative ignorance, is the stream of sin. Among these the flow of the desirables is thinned by desirelessness (वैराग्य): the flow of discrimination is rendered visible by habituating the mind to the experience of knowledge. Hence the suppression of the mental modification is dependent upon both.

तत्र स्थितौ यत्नोऽभ्यास:

(I. 13).

Of these, practice is the effect to secure steadiness. Steadiness is the undisturbed calmness of the flow of the mind, when it has become free from the modifications. Steadiness is essential for achieving success in any undertaking.

What are the obstacles that distract the mind?

The answer is given in the following *Sutra:–*

व्याधिस्त्यानंसंशयप्रमादालस्याविरतिभ्रान्तिदर्शनालब्धभूमिकत्वानवस्थितत्वानिचित्ति वक्षेपाऽन्तराया:

(Ch. I. 30).

Disease, langour, indecision, carelessness, sloth, sensuality, mistaken notion, missing the point and instability are the obstacles that cause distractions. How can the mind become pure?

मैत्रीकरुणामुदितोपेक्षाणां सुखदु:खपुण्यापुण्यविषयाणां भावनातश्चित्तप्रसादनम् ।

(Ch. I. 33).

By cultivating habits of friendliness, compassion, complacency and indifference to happiness, misery, virtue and vice the mind becomes tranquil.

तप:स्वाध्यायेश्वरप्रणिधानानि क्रियायोग:

(Ch. II, I).

Purificatory action, study and making God the motive of action is the Yoga of action.

अंहिंसाप्रातिष्ठायां तत्सन्निधौ वैरत्याग:

(Ch. II, 35).

To him, in whom the habit of not-causing injury is confirmed, no one shall be hostile. He will be loved by all.

The NYAYA-DARSHANA of Gautama is more a system of logic than of philosophy. It admits the existence of the Supreme Soul and discusses methods of reasoning. The logic is both deductive and inductive and even the most contentious dialectician cannot go any further. So subtle are the theories of Gautama. The combination of deductive particularisation and inductive generalisation reminds one of the systems of Aristotle and Mill. The VAIS'ESHIKA DARS'ANA treats of the principles of physical sciences. The fundamental principles of this system are, that all material substances are aggregates of atoms and as such aggregates they are perishable, though the atoms themselves are eternal, invisible and intangible. The aggregate may be organic or inorganic. But the subject-matter of these two treatises falls beyond the scope of our theme. Side by side with the development of these heterodox schools there arose two orthodox systems, the PURVA Mīmānsā and the UTTARA Mīmānsā. The Vedantic conception of the Supreme Spirit is the loftiest that humanity has yet been capable of. 'The Supreme Being is one, sole existent, infinite, ineffable, invariable, ruler of all, truth, wisdom, intelligence and happiness.' 'All this universe has proceeded from Him. In Him it breathes and in Him it will dissolve.' Swami S'amkarācārya is the great commentator of the Vedanta philosophy who holds that everything but *Brahma* is illusive. Brahma is only *Real*.

The ethical ideal of the *Vedanta* is indeed a high one. *These* DARS'ANAS observe a distinction in the forms of knowledge, *viz:*

(1) परविद्या—Higher knowledge which is spiritual in character and

(2) अपरविद्या—The lower knowledge of the world of sense-experience.

For spiritual enlightenment moral discipline is needed. The key-note to the practical ethics of the Vedanta whose highest ideal, is 'oneness without any distinction of I, or thou, mine, or thine.' It also means pure and disinterested love towards all. The Vedanta philosophy preaches the doctrines of *universal love*. Self-sacrifice and altruism are two other guiding rules of conduct.

'Never swerve from the path of duty,' so says the great S'amkara, and he emphasises the practice of the virtues of love, forgiveness, charity and humility. The Vedantin regards the whole universe as his own family. By the simple, pure, and chaste life he leads on this earth, he hopes, one day, to become one with God, when all his miseries shall cease and he will enjoy perfect bliss. 'Live for others' is his motto here.

Doctor Paul Deussen has made some significant remarks on the Vedanta Philosophy:–

'Love your neighbour as yourselves.' But why? By the order of nature I feel pain and pleasure only in myself not in my neighbour. The answer is in the Veda: it is in the great formulae *'Tat Tvam Ast.'* which gives in three words metaphysics and morals all together. You shall love your neighbour as yourselves because you are your neighbour and mere illusion makes you believe that your neighbour is something different from yourselves. He who knows, in the words of Gītā, himself in every thing and every thing in himself will not injure himself by himself, न हिंसति आतमाना आत्मानं. He feels himself as every thing, so he will not desire anything, for he has whatever can be had—he feels himself as every thing—so, he will not injure any body.

The Vedanta in its unfalsified form is the strongest support of pure morality and is the greatest consolation in the sufferings of life and death. Ye Indian keep to it!'

Chapter IV

Ethics of Manu

❦

M anu, the great Hindu Law-giver, is styled as the Progenitor of the whole Aryan race. His SMRITI—Code of Laws—is indeed a remarkable book and therein, the great thinker has touched upon various problems that are awaiting solution even in the twentieth century. It is probable that a reader with a 'critical bend of mind' may not fall in with all the views of Manu. All the same, Manu in an admirable way discusses the problems of education, of sanitation, of the different forms of government, of domestic and public life of a citizen and of the duties and responsibilities of four VARNAS and AS'RAMAS. There can be no denying the fact that his SMRITI is a very valuable treatise on the science of Social Organisation. True it is that, in it, as in so many other Sanskrit works, there are many interpolations and an unsympathetic reader traces out many S'LOKAS containing contradictory statements. But it must be admitted that the spirit of the book as a whole is ennobling and many sublime thoughts are embodied in it. Ideals of education and morality, at any rate, are certainly noble. Sometimes they set us thinking as to whether we are really in advance of, or have traced our steps backwards from his ideals. Many a time we are driven to the irresistible conclusion that Manu is a rationalist and if, in future, an association, like the R.P.A. of England were to be started in India, the promoters can easily lay their hands on MANU-SMRITI and issue 'a cheap reprint' of the same to give a wider publicity to the writings of an Indian philosopher and thinker. His ideal of conduct in life is not an ideal for a particular country: race, or period of life, but is one worth striving for and dying for by all right-thinking men in all ages and climes. The development of virtues which he has enumerated bears a stamp of deep erudition and profound thinking. His one SHLOKA, which we quote below, is the quintessence of the science of Ethics, or DHARMA. When we see that, within such a small compass, he has packed in much of sense and wisdom, we pay homage to the genius of that philosopher-statesman of the Vedic age. Says Manu:–

धृति: क्षमादमोऽस्तेयं शौचमिन्द्रियनिग्रह: ।
धीर्विद्या सत्यमक्रोधो दशकं धर्मलक्षणम् ॥

Manu, VI. 92.

'Courage, Forgiveness, Control of mind, Avoidance of misappropriation. Purity of mind and body, the Bringing of senses under effective control. Intellect Learning, Truthfulness and Absence of anger—these ten are the characteristics of virtue of good conduct.'

This classification enables us to see how these virtues grow and gradually come to be recognised in the development of human life. Here we see courage topping the list and none can question the position it occupies. For success in life, the possession of this virtue is a supreme necessity. Without this no movement can prosper and no achievement is possible: The sun never sets on the dominions of the Britons because of the indomitable courage of the English *Men of action*. In primitive times, this virtue was required to be shown on the battlefield, but even now, in all the departments of human activity, the importance of this virtue has ever remained the same. When a social reformer places his finger on the plague-spots of society, or when a scientist discovers a new theory, the first virtue he is required to summon to his aid, is courage, which then goes by the name of *moral courage.*

Courage gives victory and victory leads on to power. Then it is, that one gets greater chances of showing clemency to one's subordinates. Mercy, therefore, which is 'an attribute of God Himself,' should be shown to those that deserve it. Power or position in life brings in wealth and its charms are likely to lead the possessor astray. Exercise, therefore, 'Control of mind.' Deprive not others of their wealth or any other material possession. The world is full of temptations and more so, for a wealthy man. Maintain, therefore, purity of body and mind, or else, you will come to grief. With all these the training of the intellect is a great necessity, without which criminality increases, as it is a disease of the brain. Truth and absence of anger, too, are of paramount importance. They lead on to tranquility and happiness in the society as a whole. Verily these are the Ten Commandments worthy to be written in letters of gold on the grateful hearts of *Manujas*—men.

1. Water washes off bodily impurities. Mind is exalted by truthfulness. The human soul is elevated by knowledge and performance of genuine penance, and intellect is refined by noble ideas.

    (V. 109.)

What is *Dharma?* The rationalist Manu answers thus:

2. Understand that that is *Dharma*—conduct in life—which is followed by really learned men, who are free from arrogance, inordinate affection and hatred, and that which is approved by conscience.

    (II, 1.)

Where is the seat of authority? Manu answers:

(3. The seat of authority for what is moral lies in (1) Revelation, (2) Tradition, (3) On the behaviour of good people, and lastly, (4) On the inward satisfaction of conscience. (Here is a combination of the well-known methods of test).

Undoubtedly this is an appeal to the supremacy of *Reason* to establish 'a system of ethics verifiable by experience, independent of arbitrary assumption.'

4. Freedom from inflicting pain to others, truthfulness, honesty, purity, control of senses is a short form of the law of guidance to all the four divisions of society.

(X. 63.)

5. Let those that seek happiness be content. Contentment is at the basis of happiness and mean ambition gives rise to misery.

(IV. 12.)

6. Speak the truth. Let it not be unpleasant. Speak not a pleasing falsehood. This is the ancient rule.

(IV. 138.)

7. Let not a wise man care much for honour and mind at all dishonour. Else his peace of mind will be disturbed.

(IV. 162.)

8. Hospitable treatment of a deserving guest gives wealth, fame, long life and happiness.

(III. 106.)

9. Dependence or slavery is miserable. Independence gives happiness. (Learn self-help and hanker not after mean flattery or degrading service).

(IV. 160.)

10. Perform only such deeds as would be applauded by your conscience. Avoid others.

(IV. 161.)

11. Good conduct is the grand rule of life.

(I. 108.)

12. Teacher is the personification of a learned man. Father represents Brahma, the Creator and Mother is compared to the Earth, inasmuch as she feeds us and looks to all our comforts. Brother is like our own self. Try your best to please all these at all times. Looking to their comforts is in itself a penance. Consult them before you perform any action. (Revere thy father, mother, brother and teacher.)

II. 225, 228–29.

13. When a guest* comes to you, treat him hospitably by giving him a proper seat, water to wash his feet and food, to the extent to which your means permit.

14. In the house of a good man there may not be anything, but at least you will find these certainly, *viz.*, a plot of ground to sit upon, good water and kind speech.

(III. 101.)

15. The murder of a learned man, the drinking of wine, the misappropriation of another's wealth, and treating with disrespect the wife, or the person of a teacher are great sins. Avoid them.

(XI. 55.)

In the succeeding S'LOKAS he has defined, in more explicit terms, each of these 'great sins' and has included the following also among them:– (1) Deserting parents, (2) Offering one's children for sale, (3) Deforesting a forest by hewing down trees. Then follows a long list of minor sins.

---

* अतिथि a guest is one who has no fixed time for visiting, who does not remain long in a house and who is wise, considerate and deserving of help. (II. 102).

16. Repentance followed by a strong determination, 'never to repeat the evil action', purifies one of sins.

(XI. 231.)

17. Granting that an evil deed has been committed, either, through ignorance, or knowing that it is a sin, the only way to be relieved of it, is not to do that act a second time.(XI. 233.)

18. Acquisition of knowledge is penance to a Brahmin (learned man). Protecting the weak is the duty of a Kshatriya (brave man). Adding to the material prosperity of his country is the duty of a merchant. Ministering to the needs of these three is the duty of a S'udra, one who is by nature unfit to do any other work.

(II. 236.)

19. A man learned in sciences destroys all sins by the force of his intellect, just as fire consumes all fuel in an instant.

(XI. 247.)

20. Study of the Vedas, austerity, wisdom, purity, control of the senses, performances of good deeds and contemplation of the self are the qualities of a SATVIKA soul. Eagerness to commence a work but unsteadiness in its performance, persistence in doing forbidden acts, and slavish adherence to sense-pleasures are the usual characteristics of RAJASIC people. Avarice, addiction to too much sleep, forgetfulness, cruelty, disbelief in God, ficklemindedness, parasitism and infatuation are the features of TAMASIC men.

(XII. 31-33.)

21. He, who considers all sentient beings as worthy of love, and equal to his own self and who is cosmopolitan in views, obtains salvation.

(XII. 91.)

Chapter IV

ॐ

The Ethics of Manu.
Sanskrit Shlokas:–

1. अद्धर्गात्राणि शुध्यन्ति मन: सत्येन शुध्यति ।
   विद्यातपोभ्यां भूतात्मा बुद्धिर्ज्ञानेन शुध्यति ॥

2. बुद्धद्धि: सेवित: सद्धिर्नित्यमद्वेषरागिभि: ।
   ह्येनाभ्यनुज्ञातो यो धर्मस्तन्निबोधत ॥

3. श्रुति: स्मृति: सदाचारो स्वस्य च प्रियमात्मन: ।

4. अंहिसा सत्यमस्तेयं शौचमिन्द्रियानेग्रह: ।
   एतं सामांसिकं धर्मं चातुर्वर्ण्येऽब्रवीन्मनु: ॥

5. संतोषं परमास्थाय सुखार्थी संयतो भवेत् ।
   संतोषमूलं हि सुखं दु:खमूलं विपर्यय: ॥

6. सत्यं ब्रूयात् प्रियं ब्रूयान्न ब्रूयात् सत्यमप्रियम् ।
   प्रियं च नानृतं ब्रूयादेष धर्म: सनातन: ॥

7. संमानाद्ब्रह्माणो नित्यमुद्विजेत विषादिव ।
   अमृतस्येव चाकाङ्क्षेद्वमानम्य सर्वदा ॥

8. धन्यं यशस्यमापुष्यं स्वर्ग्यं वातिथिपूजनम् ।

9. सर्वं परवशं दु:खं सर्वमात्मवशं सुखम् ।

10. यत्कर्मकुर्वतोऽस्य स्यात् परितोषोऽन्तरात्मन: ।
    तत्प्रयत्नेन कुर्वीत विपरीतं तु वर्जयेत् ॥

11. आचार: परमो धर्म: ॥

12. आचार्यो ब्रह्माणो मूर्ति: पिता मूर्ति: प्रजापते: ।
    माता पृथिव्या मूर्तिस्तु भ्राता स्वो मूर्तिरात्मन: ।

तयोर्नित्यं प्रियं कुर्यादाचार्यस्य च सर्वदा ।
तेष्वेव त्रिषु तुष्टेषु तप: सर्वं समाप्तये ।
तेषां त्रयाणां शुश्रूषा परमं तप उच्यते ।
न तैरनभ्यनुज्ञातो धर्ममन्यं समाचरेत् ॥

13. संप्राप्ताय त्वतिथये प्रदद्यादासनोदके ।
अन्नं चैव यथा शक्ति सत्कृत्य विधिपूर्वकम् ॥

14. तृणानि भूमिरुदकं वाक् चतुर्थी च मूनृता ।
एतान्यपि सतां गेहे नोच्छिद्यन्ते कदाचन ॥

15. ब्रह्महत्या सुरापानं स्तेयं गुर्वङ्गनागम: ।
महान्ति पापकान्याहु: संसर्गश्चापि तै: सह ॥

16. कृत्वा पापं हि संतप्य तस्मात् पापात् प्रमुच्यते ।
नैवं कुर्यां पुनरिति निवृत्त्या पूयते तु स: ॥

17. अज्ञानाद्यदि वा ज्ञात्वा कृत्वा कर्म विगर्हितम् ।
तस्माद्विमुक्तिमान्वेच्छन्द्वितीयं न समाचरेत् ॥

18. ब्राह्मणभ्य तपो ज्ञानं तप: क्षत्रस्य लक्षणम् ।
वैश्यस्य तु तपो वार्ता तप: शूद्रस्य सेवनम् ॥

19. यथैधस्तेजंसा वह्नि: प्राप्तं निर्दहति क्षणात् ।
तथा ज्ञानाग्निना पापं सर्वं दहति वेदवित् ॥

20. वेदाभ्यासस्तपो ज्ञानं शौचामेन्द्रियनिग्रह: ।
धर्मक्रियात्मचिन्ता च सात्त्विकं गुलक्षणम् ॥,
आरम्भरुचिता धैर्यमसत्कार्यपरिग्रह: ।
विषयोपसेवा चाजस्रं राजसं गुणलक्षणम् ॥
लोभ: स्वप्रोऽधृति: क्रैर्यं नास्तिक्यं भिन्नवृत्तिता
याचिष्णुता प्रमादश्च तामसं गुलक्षणम् ॥

21. सर्वभूतेषु चात्मानं सर्वभूतानि चात्माने ।
समं पश्यन् आत्मयाजी स्वाराजयमधिराच्छति ॥

Chapter V

Ethics of Vālmiki

❧

In the whole range of Sanskrit literature, if there is any work, at the mere mention of which, a thrilling sensation of joy and reverence runs through the veins of an Indian, it is the RAMAYANA, the immortal work of the immortal Valmiki. In its literary grandeour, and in its historical significance, it has no parallel. Its style is so simple and charming, so fluent and chaste that any reader possessing an ordinary knowledge of the Sanskrit language, can fully grasp the meaning and thought, and enter into the spirit, of the author. In the choice of suitable words and expressions, Valmiki is always precise and perspicuous, in the richness of imagery and the selection of beautiful similes, he has no equal. The condensed style and the sublime theme are so delightful, that, every time we read and ponder over those stanzas which are rich in thought and expression, new beauties are discovered and grand ideas are suggested. The natural scenes are so vividly and accurately described and the human characters are so ably and wonderfully delineated that a reader, no matter what his caste, colour or creed be, cannot remain without paying a great homage to the great celestial poet. We, mortals, who are panting after transient joys and ephemeral gains of the world, we, the worshippers of Mammon, who are tossed hither and thither on the waves of the stormy ocean of life, we, the strenuous fighters of this battle of life, who at times become disgusted at not finding an iota of true peace and harmony, we, frail human beings, would do well to drink deep at the fountain of the ADI-KAVI and then, we shall feel ourselves slowly rising above this sensuous plane. When we bestow mature consideration on some of the episodes of the RAMAYANA, we shall clearly see how men are made and unmade and how empires are built and ruined.

From Kashmir to Comorin, from Karachi to Calcutta, Śri Rama's name is a household word. When a man, after a hard day's work, returns home and stretches himself on his bed to enjoy his hard-earned rest, he unconsciously utters 'Rama, Rama, and feels, as if all his troubles are at an end. When the dead body of a dear friend, or, a near relative, is being carried to the funeral ground the words commonly uttered are 'Ram-Nam-Sat-hai.' From the cradle to the crematorium this charming word, 'Rama,' serves as a soothing balm, nay, it is believed by many, that a mere repetition of the name several times a day, purifies the soul of all sins and leads it on to beatitude. It is also the firm conviction of some parents that, in case their children were to write this name over and over again, fame and fortune will fall to their lot. Hundreds of talismans with this name written on them, are hung round the necks of many *Bhaktas* who believe, thereby, that no devil can possess them. When friends meet friends they say 'Rama, Rama.' Those medicines whose efficacy is believed to be marvellous are described as RAMABANA AUSHADHAS. The walls of certain houses are beautifully painted and this charming little word 'Sri Rama, Jaya-Rama' is written on them and it is expected that in such houses peace and plenty will always reign. On marriage and other festive occasions when friends and relatives dine together, they, with one voice cry aloud saying, 'SITA-KANTA-SMARANA-JAYA-RAMA', only to offer their thanks even in those joyous moments, to the Almighty. When professional bards conduct their KATHAS, and raise the feeling of piety in the audience to the highest pitch, they, in unison, clap their hands and say 'Rama, Rama, and Rama,' and the whole amphitheatre rings with the music of their voice. A professional beggar, besmearing his body with ashes, goes on repeating this name in the streets, at times wallowing in the mud, all the while crying out 'Rama, Rama, Sītarama,' and thus moves even a miser to part with his favourite *Kowri*. A forlorn Hindu sadhu knocks at the door of a householder saying 'Sita-Rama'; and forthwith, the *Grihini* proceeds to dole out a handful of rice to him, only to honour Sita, the idol of her heart and to revere the blessed memory of her pet Sita's husband, Rama. Above all, Rama is believed to be the incarnation of Vishnu, the all-pervading Deity, who came to this world to re-establish the reign of justice and uprightness. Even the modern-day reformers, revivalists and rationalists too who are not prepared to accept the theory of incarnation, in any case, believe that Rama was a great personage and that, even in these degenerate days, when hero-worship, in the true sense of the word, has become a thing of the past, Śri Ramas's memory deserves to be kept green. Unless there is some extraordinary halo of greatness round the great personality, his name cannot wield such a great influence as this on the minds of peasants and princess alike even to this day. Professor Weber is of opinion that the principal characters in the RAMAYANA are not historical personages but mere personifications of certain events and circumstances. The Sita (Furrow), he says, occurs both in the Rig-Veda and Grihya-Sūtra. The Furrow is an object of worship and represents Aryan agriculture. But many scholars, after a patient research and careful examination of circumstantial evidence, have arrived at the conclusion that the story of the

Rāmāyana is based on solid facts of history. There is no doubt that in the Rāmāyana, historical truth is interwoven with myth, and in certain passages the poet Vālmīki, who seems to have an inordinate love for exaggeration, has freely indulged in the use of hyperbole, and his fertile brain makes stones float in water and mountains fly in air. Even granting for a moment that the Rāmāyana is an allegory of 'The Ploughman and the Furrow', the loftiness of its ethics and the sublimity of the theme shall ever remain the same. Call the RAMAYANA by any name, and like a rose it is bound to smell as sweet.

Man is a social being and his everyday life is associated with the paid or the unpaid services of his fellow creatures. If we are to fight this battle of life successfully, it should be our first and foremost duty to know how we ought to conduct ourselves towards our relatives, friends, superiors and subordinates. Failure in realising our responsibility in that direction means an utter failure in life also. In the RAMAYANA, both by sound precepts and noble examples, we are taught how, as sons, we are to obey our parents, how, as brothers, we should love one another, how, as friends, we should help one another, how, as servants, we should serve our masters and how, as rulers, we should govern the subject races. In this topsy-turvy world of ours, not unoften occasions arise when, even the bravest and the wisest are baffled in their attempts to chalk out a right path for themselves and at such a critical juncture, the study of the RAMAYANA would inspire them with zeal and enthusiasm.

Rama, an Ideal Son

Obedience to elders is one of the virtues, which young students ought to cultivate and Rāma was fully endowed with that virtue. King Daśaratha who somehow fell a victim to the jealousy, shrewdness and selfishness of his wife Kaikayī, issues the mandate that the prince Rāma should be banished and be deprived of all the benefits accruing to him as the crowned monarch of Ayodhyā. Why does Rāma go into voluntary exile, though all the people there, assembled to pronounce benedictions on him, dissuade him from doing so? Why does he prefer wilderness to the pomp of sovereignty? What charms could asceticism have for a prince? Is it because, three thousand years ago, civilisation had fewer attractions and Ayodhyā and the Dandaka forest were one and the same? Yes, to be sure, there were in the palace no thundering motor cars, brilliant electric *pankhas,* sparkling soda water, delicious lemonade, and crystalline ice, but according to the conditions and circumstances peculiar to those times there were articles of luxury, such as ornamental umbrellas and tempting *Rathas,* which could have enticed the prince. In his case it must be admitted that a sense of stern duty and strict obedience to his father alone compelled him to prefer a forest to a palace. When Bharata, his younger brother approached him with a request to return to Ayodhyā Rāma remarked:–

यद्ब्रवीन्मां नरलाकसत्कृतः
पिता महात्मा विबुधाधिपोपमः
तदेव मन्ये परमात्मनो हितं
न सर्वलोकेश्वरभावमव्ययम् ॥

'Whatever my father, who is loved and respected by the people, who is noble-minded and wise, commands, that, I consider to be conducive to my welfare. And to me the sovereignty of the world is nothing.' If there is a Casabianca for the English youth, that brave lad who allowed his body to be consumed by fire, simply to obey his father, for the Hindu youth there is certainly a Rāma, an ideal son, who abdicated his throne and sacrificed all the comforts of his life, when he once realised that obedience is the virtue of virtues.

Rama, an Ideal Ruler

When the time came for Rama to hold the reins of government, he ruled wisely and sympathetically. He respected public opinion to such an extent that even one word of censure, spoken by a washerman who condemned him for having brought his wife back from the abode of Rāvaṇa, was sufficient for him to be on his guard. All his subjects looked upon him as their father. His reign was one of sympathy and of justice 'seasoned with mercy.' Even when Rāvaṇa was vanquished, he chose his brother Bibhīshaṇa as his successor and all the feudatory princes were as strictly loyal to him as they ought to have been. Sympathy was the keynote of his rule. His policy of non-annexation of a conqured country is an eternal challenge of Indian culture to the land-greed of nations.

Lakshmaṇa, an Ideal Brother

Lakshmaṇa is one of the most remarkable characters in this great epic. Voluntarily he accompanies his brother in exile, suffers all privations for his sake, at times takes no proper food, shares all his elder brother's miseries, nobly fights by his side and returns to Ayodhyā to assist his royal brother in his beneficent rule. Some ingenious writer has suggested that Lakshmaṇa, the ideal brother, deserves to be the hero of RAMAYANA and there is much truth in this opinion. In times of difficulties, when Sītā is alone in the forest, he keeps a constant watch over her. There is a peculiarly interesting episode, which clearly brings his nobility of character into greater relief. In the diligent but heartrending search for Sītā in the forest, it is said that Rama came across a few jewels belonging to Sītā which he could not easily identify. Forthwith Rāma asks Lakshmaṇa whether he could recognise them. The younger brother respectfully answers:– 'My sovereign lord, I am quite unable to identify them but I can only say that one particular ornament belongs to her and that is the one which she wore on her legs. I saw the same when I used to prostrate myself at her feet.' The character of Bharata, too, is equally noble. He was not at all anxious to be the ruler when his eldest brother had better claims. All the way he went to the forest, begged of his brother to return to Ayodhyā and when he found him obdurate, he brought his brother's sandals, placed them on the throne and governed the country in his name. In the world's history, we search in vain to find two such noble princely brothers.

Sita, an Ideal Wife

Of the female characters Sītā is indeed the noblest. Her sincere love for Rama is simply unparalleled. She was the daughter of a king and the wife to the son of a king. Her mother-in-law and husband too, dissuaded her from leading the life of a hermit in the forest. She sternly refused to do so and remarked, 'I shall follow my husband, nay, I shall lead the way in the dense jungles, removing the thorns in the way of my lord.'

Rāvaṇa offers her temptations and promises to make her his queen. She becomes indignant and cries out, 'Oh, you villain, bear in mind that chastity is a very strong armour of mine and it is proof against your vain glory and mean power. You can do me no harm. I care not for your pelf and power.'

Hanuman's Faithful Service

If there was any servant who, through thick and thin, stood by his master, that was Hanuman. It was he who, in spite of great obstacles, first discovered Sītā, rendered a yeoman's service to Rāma in his mighty war with the Rakhasas and saved the life of Lakshmaṇa when he received a deadly wound. Hanuman's whole life is one of loyal and disinterested service to his sovereign lord. One incident in his life may deserve a passing notice. It is remarked that Rama, after his coronation, distributed presents to several of his men but gave nothing to Hanuman. Sītā, who was closely watching the proceedings was greatly astonished at this strange behaviour of her husband and remarked 'How is it, my Lord, that you have set aside the claims of our loyal subject Māruti?' Rama in all sincerity replied, 'My dear, his services to me and to my cause are so great that I do not know how adequately to reward him and hence my silence.'

Mark, patient reader, the ingenuity of Vālmīki. In one story, call it historical or allegorical, he has preached the sublimest and the most practical principles of ethics. Hence, it is that among the Sanskrit-knowing, the name of that celestial poet and among the Hindi-knowing, the name of TULASIDASA are household words. Kālidāsa has immortalised the names of the sovereigns of the illustrious line of the 'Solar-kings' in his RAGHUVAMSA. He has, in one ŚLOKA admirably summarised the salient features of these kings,

शैशवेऽभ्यस्तविद्यानां यौवने विषयैषिणाम् ।
वार्द्धक्ये मुनिवृत्तीनां योगेनान्ते तनुत्यजाम् ॥

Raghuvamsa I.

'In their boyhood they diligently studied and received education. In manhood they ruled well and cared for their worldly prosperity. In their old age they led the life of ascetics (life of service to humanity at large), and ended their glorious careers after the manner of a *Yogin,* by becoming one with the Universal Spirit.' Indeed the names of the kings of the type of Dilīpa, Daśaratha and Rāma are names to conjure with, and so are those of Vālmīki and Kālidāsa. the two great Indian poets, who have rendered their lives more illustrious and more worthy of imitation by their splendid poems, but for whose laudable efforts, these names would have been lost in the haze of antiquity.

Chapter VI

Ethics of the Mahabharata

❦

The MAHABHARATA is a great Hindu epic, which throws a flood of light on the development of ethical ideas in ancient India. As the term implies, it treats of the history of the kings of the family of *Bharata,* the son of *Dushyanta* the hero of the famous drama of ŚAKUNTALA, composed by Kālidāsa, the prince of Indian poets. The KAURAVAS and the PANDAVAS had the honour to belong to this illustrious family, which after the great and disastrous war became practically extinct, and with it set the glorious sun of Vedic religion and learning. Tradition ascribes the authorship of this book to VYASA. It is divided into eighteen chapters, each of which is called a *Paroan* named after the incident narrated in that particular chapter. The following are the names of the *Paroas:*–

1. ĀDI-PARVA – in which a commencement is made to narrate the history of the PANDAVAS and the KAURAVAS.
2. SABHA-PARVA—in which is given an account of the three well-known meetings.
3. VANA-PARVA—in which is described the life in the forest led by the Pāndavas.
4. VIRATA-PARVA—in which is narrated the kind of *incognito* life led by the Pāndavas at the palace of king Virata.

5. UDYOGA-PARVA—in which is given the account of the life-and-death struggle carried on by the Pāndavas to regain their kingdom from the usurpers.

6. BISHMA-PARVA—which relates the history of the war waged by Bhīshma with the Pāndavas.

7. DRONA-PARVA—wherein Drona assumes the command and fights with the Pāndavas.

8. KARNA-PARVA—which relates to the fight of Karna.

9. ŚALYA-PARVA—in which the account of the fight by Śalya is given.

10. SAUPTIK-PARVA—wherein ASVATHAMA'S night siege is described.

11. STRI-PARVA—a chapter of mourning by the wives of the Kauravas.

12. SHANTI-PARVA—describes the times of peace.

13. ANUSASANA-PARVA—wherein is given the advice of BHISHMA-PITA to the Pāndavas.

14. ASVA-MEDHA-PARVA—describes the Aśvamedha sacrifice of the Pāndavas and their victory.

15. ASRAMA-VASIKA-PARVA—describes the forest life of Dhṛitarāshtra and Vidura.

16. MAUSALA-PARVA—describes the miracles of a pounder.

17. MAHA-PRASTHANIKA-PARVA—narrates the readiness of the Pāndavas to go to heaven.

18. SVARGAROHANA-PARVA—describes their ascent to heaven.

A critical study of the book as a whole enables a student to realise the economic, political, intellectual and religious condition of the epic age of the Hindu history, and, though there are many episodes and philosophic disquisitions scattered all over the book, to an ethicist the study of Vana-parva, Udyoga-parva, Śanti-parva and Anuśāsana-parva affords food for reflection. Brushing aside the mythical cobwebs ingeniously spun by the poet, and extricating oneself from the labyrinth of poetic imagination and speculation, one can feel the permanent impressions left by moral philosophy on the characters of this great Hindu epic.

The *summum-bonum* of the Indian philosophers was the ultimate union of the human soul with the Divine and for this union, renunciation of the world was by some considered an absolute necessity. But it was held by another set of thinkers that this attainment was compatible with the life of righteousness led in this world and that there was no need at all for the giving-up of all connections with the worldly activities. The Mahābhārata and pre-eminently the Bhagavad-gītā preach, in quite unequivocal terms, this philosophy of action. It must, however, be admitted that there are some ŚLOKAS which propound a diametrically opposite view, *viz.,* that of renunciation. Kṛshna, the towering personality, and Yudhishṭhira, an embodiment of piety and righteousness, are very interesting characters. Every episode and every character has its own moral to point. The contrast between Yudhishṭhira and Duryodhana, Vidura and Śakuni, Bhīma and Duhśāsana and, Karna and Arjuna, is as remarkable as it is striking. The life of every character is full of grand lessons and every reader can take a leaf out of the life-history of these wonderful personages and chalk out a path of righteousness for himself.

Bhīshma's frankness, his discharge of duties for duty's sake, his unflinching devotion to truth and God; Yudhishṭhira's love of truth, his equanimity of temper in times of difficulties, his simplicity of character even at the zenith of his material prosperity, and his gentle words which would turn away the wrath of Bhīma and Arjuna; Bhīma's gigantic strength, never used as that of a giant, his reverence for preceptors and elders; Arjuna's keen penetrating intellect, his perseverance and steadiness, and his love of righteousness and dutiful behaviour towards Kṛshna; Kṛshna's diplomacy coupled with tact and intelligence, his loyal adherence to the cause of righteousness; Draupadī's fortitude, her skill in the management of household affairs, her counsels of wisdom to her husband and her courage in times of difficulties are all remarkably illustrated in this epic. In direct contrast to these, the treachery, the want of foresight, selfishness, the spirit of self-aggrandizement and deceit, perjury and chicanery, which formed the weapons offensive and defensive of the Kauravas, are also noteworthy. The civil war gave a deathblow not only to the family of the Kurus, but also gave a setback to the civilisation and progress which was the outcome of Vedic religion and philosophy.

In the *Vana-parva,* the Rshi MARKANDEYA gives the following piece of advice to the Pāndavas:–

'Love all sentient beings; Speak the truth; Be humble; Control your passions; As kings work for the welfare of subjects; Propitiate gods and fathers; Abandon pride; Attain purity of speech and action, without which there can be no penance; He, who speaks wisely and acts wisely, is a saint. Love righteousness. Be straightforward and courageous.'

In the same *parva* we come across the following dialogue between Yaksha and Yudhishthira. Yaksha asks him questions and he replies:

Q. What is the eternal *dharma?*
A. The attainment of emancipation from the turmoils of the world by leading a virtuous life.
Q. How can fame be attained?
A. By means of discriminate charity.
Q. What is the key to heaven and happiness ?
A. A life of rectitude and truthfulness.
Q. Which is the best way of earning money?
A. Honesty and straightforwardness in our dealings.
Q. Which is the best wealth?
A. Knowledge.

Q. Which is the best acquisition?

A, Acquisition of good health.

Q. Which is the best happiness?

A. Contentment.

Q. Which is the virtue of virtues?

A. Mercy.

Q Whose company is to be sought?

A. The company of the pious.

Q. Which man is the beloved of all?

A. A man free from egotism and selfishness.

Q. How can man become happy?

A. By abandoning greed.

Q. What are penance, forgiveness, knowledge and mercy?

A. Discharge of legitimate duty is penance. Love of truth is knowledge. Wishing the good of all is mercy.

Q. Who is a good man?

A. One who, day and night, thinks of doing good to others.

Q. Define charity, wisdom, folly, fate and cruelty.

A. Protection given to sentient beings is charity. Knowledge of *dharma* is wisdom. Ignorance of God is folly. Fate is the resultant of good deeds and good disposition. Speaking ill of others is cruelty.

Q. Who goes to hell?

A. He goes to hell, who having wealth, does not make a proper use of it; he goes to hell, who does not revere the Vedas, the elders and other Sat-Sāstras.

Q. What gives real Brahminhood?

A. A man does not become a Brahmin by the mere study of the Vedas and by the mere fact of his having been born in a noble family. But it is good character alone that makes him a Brahmin. A man, though he be a profound scholar of the Veda, is worse than a ŚUDRA, if his behaviour be not in confromity with the rules of good conduct.

In the Anuśāsana-parva Bhīshmāchārya gives the following piece of advice to the PANDAVAS.

'It is the sacred duty of the Kshatriyas to fight bravely and die for the cause of righteousness.'

Speaking of the attributes of a king he says:–

'A king must govern according to the strict rules of equity, he must look upon the subjects as his own children, he must be active, a lover of truth, his justice must be seasoned with mercy, and he must be liberal minded and must be a patron of learning.'

As for the subjects he says:–

'They must be prepared to die for their king and kingdom, and they must be strictly loyal to the king and his government.'

Action versus Fate:– Industry and labour alone are to be depended upon. There is nothing like *fate*. Fate means nothing more than the result of the actions done in the past birth. If the actions are good fate will be good. We must be doing good deeds so that at least, in our future birth we may be happy.

Penance, he adds, consists in compassion and love of truth and in doing good to others. Mere fasting and subjecting the body to pain can never be penance.

Duties of Students:– Speaking of these, he says, 'Revere and obey your preceptors and parents. A teacher is in many respects superior to parents in as much as he gives one spiritual and mental strength.'

Characteristics of Dharma:– Of these, he observes, that DAYA—mercy—is the basis. Loving others as we do ourselves and good conduct are the essentials.

Speaking of God, he says:–

'God is omnipresent and omniscient. He is the Merciful Power and Supporter of the Universe. We are all "images of God." We should attain purity of mind, speech and strive to attain Him. Our vicious deeds take us far away from this fountain of bliss. Love Him with all thy heart.'

Bhīshmāchārya's advice is in itself a treatise on ethics. We have given above only a few extracts. With such noble words on his lips he is said to have shaken off the mortal coil. Next to Śrī Kṛshṇa, he stands in the whole Mahābhārata as the great propounder of moral philosophy. Yudhishṭhira in an admirable way sums up the truth. In his exile he addresses the queen:–

धर्मो नित्यः सुखदुःखे त्वनित्ये
जीवो नित्यस्तस्य हेतुस्त्वनित्य ॥

'I follow *Dharma* not because I see any immediate profit from it, but from a conviction that virtue is to be followed for its *own sake.*'

The following ŚLOKA from the Mahābhārata is indeed memorable:

धर्मं चरामि सुश्रेणि न धमफलकारणात् ।
धर्मवाणिज्यको हीनो जघन्यो धर्मवादिनाम् ॥
न जातु कामान्न भयान्न लोभाद् ।
धम त्यजेत् जीवितस्यापि हेतोः ॥

'Give up not righteousness for greed or fear
Or for desire, or for even life's dear sake.
Eternal's virtue, pain and pleasure fleeting,
Fleeting is life, but not the soul divine.'

(Mr C.V. Vaidya's rendering).

Chapter VII

Ethics of Vidura

༄

Vidura-Niti forms a part of the Mahābhārata and is included in the *Udyogaparva*. Vidura, a philosopher-statesman living at the court of king Dhritarāshtra, is the author of this *niti*. The King-Emperor Dhritarāshtra speaks of him as 'MAHAPRAJNA' and 'DIRGHA-DARSHI', meaning thereby that he was very wise and sagacious. The style of the *niti* is characteristic of the classic period of Sanskrit literature, and the sublimity of the thoughts expressed therein is only equalled by the greatness of the theme. The book is divided into eight chapters and contains about 500 *shlokas*. In the course of a conversation with *Dhritarashtra*, Vidura first mentions the attributes of a Pandit, *i.e.*, a learned man.

Says he:–

1. He who performs good deeds and hates all that is evil, who is a firm believer in God, and whose attachment to goodness is intense, is a Pandit.

2. He who does not possess anger, pride, impulsive nature, and who does not think too much of himself, is a Pandit.

3. He who, in the discharge of his duties, remains uninfluenced, either by heat or cold or by prosperity or adversity, is a Pandit.

4. He, who listens attentively for a long time and understands or grasps the meaning quickly, who is not avaricious and who is of a non-interfering nature is a Pandit.

5. Those men, who aspire not for things unattainable ... who never cry for the moon ... who grieve not for things that have already happened and cannot be mended ... who do not cry over spilt milk ... and who do not lose the equilibrium of their minds in times of distress ... are wise men.

6. Those, who take delight in the doing of noble deeds and do only such acts as go to the advancement of prosperity, and who do not feel jealous of others, are, O King, learned men.

7. He, who understands the secrets of all sciences relating to the development of the whole animal creation, who thoroughly recognises the secrets of success in any undertaking, and is ingenious in the study of human nature, is a Pandit.

8. He, who neglects the performance of his own duties, and puts obstacles in the way of others, and who proves faithless to a friend, is styled a fool.

9. An uninvited guest, a garrulous person making uncalled-for remarks, a person placing confidence in a treacherous person, all these become contemptible.

10. He, who, having obtained immense wealth and education, leads a life of simplicity, is a wise man.

11. What man is more despicable than the one who, having neglected the welfare of his dependents, leads an easy going merry life?

12. An arrow discharged from a bow may or may not kill anybody. But a wise man, taking leave of his common-sense, is sure to bring ruin upon his own country and king.

13. Truth is like a ladder leading to heaven, or like a boat enabling one to cross this ocean of misery.

14. Only one defect can be ascribed to persons having the quality of mercy enthroned in their hearts. People consider them weakminded.

15. This is not in reality the weakness of these men. Mercy is in itself power. Even to weak persons it is an attribute. It is an ornament to the brave.

16. The quality of mercy can control the universe. There is nothing that cannot be accomplished by this. A wicked man even cannot inflict any injury on one in whose hands there is the defensive weapon of mercy.

17. Duty alone is religion. Mercy alone is tranquillity. Education is the only contentment. Mercy to sentient beings brings ultimate happiness.

18. These three are the gates leading to hell:–
    (1) Lust. (2) Anger. (3) Avarice. Therefore avoid them.

19. A man desiring prosperity ought to abandon these vicious habits:– (1) Excessive sleep; (2) Idleness: (3) Fear: (4) Anger: and (5) Dilatoriness.

20. He is the best man who has no pride, no jealousy, no hatred towards the king, no malignant nature, and who does not keep company with wicked men.

21. No evil falls to the lot of him who is moderate in eating, who distributes things among his dependents proportionately and who helps even an enemy deserving aid.

22. One, who desires to be prosperous in this world, should partake of wholesome and easily degestible food.

23. *Dharma* is protected by truth, education is retained by concentration of mind, beauty by careful washing and family is guarded by good character.

24. In my opinion, a man destitute of good deeds though born in a noble family is of no consequence, while a man with good character, though born among the low castes, deserves respect.

25. Education, wealth and birth in a high family are harmful in the case of a wicked man, while they are very useful for a noble-minded being.

26. Character is the noblest possession of man. Without it he comes to grief. His wealth, his family and his whole life are of no avail, in case he loses his character.

27. Loss of the means of livelihood excites fear in the lowest type of man; death causes fear to one of the middle type: but to the best, loss of honour and good name gives cause for greatest sorrow and fright.

28. A forest that is cut down by axes or arrows (or by any other means of destruction) may grow again, but a bad word uttered is dangerous in consequences. A wound inflicted upon the feeling of others by the use of bad or indecent words becomes incurable.

29. The more a man endeavours to think and do good deeds the more will he be endowed with a capacity to accomplish his work. There is no doubt about this.

30. Avoid these things:– (i) The use of intoxicating drugs, (ii) Quarrelsome nature, (iii) Enmity with a nation, (iv) Creating disputes or causing quarrels between a husband and a wife, (v) Division or disunion among the members of a family, (vi) Disloyalty to a ruler.

31. Old age spoils the beauty of complexion, greed lessens courage, death deprives one of life, malignant nature spoils the *Dharma,* anger causes loss of health, service of an ignoble person degrades one's character, lust deprives one of shame, but vanity deprives one of everything.

32. These eight qualities make a man well-known:– (1) Intelligence, (2) Nobility of character, (3) Keeping the senses under one's control, (4) Study, (3) Bravery, (6) Speaking much in proper time, (7) Charity within one's means and (8) Gratefulness.

33. This is the eight-fold division of *Dharma:*– (1) Performance of sacrifice, (2) Study and concentration of mind, (3) Performance of penance, (4) Truth, (5) Forgiveness, (6) Compassion, (7) Want of greed, (8) Charity.

34. Do such actions in youth as would make you happy in old age. All through your life do those acts which would give you happiness even after death.

35. A man's character is formed by the nature of the company he keeps. He can develop it according to his will also.

36. He who always thinks of the welfare of others, and never allows himself to be influenced by ill-feelings towards others, he who is truthful, gentle in nature, controls his mind is the best type of a man.

37. Happiness and misery, birth and death, profit and loss, fall in rotation, as it were, to the lot of man. Brave men, therefore, are neither overjoyed at success nor feel depressed at defeat.

38. O King! It is very easy to find many persons who always talk sweet words. But it is extremely difficult to come across persons, who talk disagreeable words but such as really result in ultimate goodness. Fewer still are the persons who will listen to such words.

39. To a man with cleanly habits, wealth, strength and purity of body and mind come.

40. Six advantages accrue to a man eating in moderation:– (1) Health. (2) Long life, (3) Strength, (4) Happiness, (5) Healthy progeny, (6) None calling him by the contemptuous name of a glutton.

41. He who has intelligence, valour and enterprising spirit, need not be anxious about obtaining his means of livelihood.

42 Let it be remembered that the performance of good deeds alone is conducive to the welfare of human beings, failing which one will have to repent.

43. Endeavours should be made to control anger towards wise men, kings, scholars, old men, innocent children and sickly persons (patients).

44. Man is responsible for the deeds done, for the words spoken and for the thoughts entertained by him. Therefore, do and think only of good deeds.

45. *Dharma* is eternal, happiness and misery are ephemeral: Soul is eternal but body is short-lived. Think more of eternal things. Lead a life of contentment. 'Contentment alone is a continual feast.'

46. Life is a river, virtue is its bathing place, truth is its water, moral courage is its bank, mercy is the waves thereof. In such a river good men take a dip.

These are some of the *shlokas* which deal with the ethics of Vidura, who preached morality to Dhritarashtra and advocated the cause of righteousness to him. The cause of the Pandavas was the cause of righteousness. The war of the Mahabharata was a turning point in the history of Vedic India. In this civil war truth ultimately triumphed, but the effects of the war were, in many ways, disastrous. Many a noble soul fell on that fatal field of *Kurukshetra* (near Panipat) and the future was bound to be gloomy. Once again, the evil forces predominated till the advent of Lord Buddha, the embodiment of mercy. His mission was to revive the ethical spirit of true religion. That spirit breathes through this *Niti*. Buddhism is an echo of the teachings of the sublime Upanishads, and Vidura *Niti*, like so many other *Nitis*, is the essence of the ethical part of the Primitive *Hindu* Religion or better still, of the Vedic Religion. *Vidura,* the author, it is easy to perceive, lays great stress on truth, nobility of mind and the performance of duty. He also recognises that moral greatness is at the basis of individual or social greatness. He is dinning into the ears of *Dhritarashtra* the significance he ought to attach to the laws of morality in his relations with the *Pandavas*. The shrewd king who gave an indirect applause to virtue, ultimately relied upon fate and disregarded his teachings and the result was that he and his party met with a disastrous downfall which they so richly deserved. The fall of the *Kauravas,* we repeat, sounds a note of warning to those that disregard the principles of equity. The triumph of the *Pandavas* who were numerically inferior to the *Kauravas* is triumph for the cause of righteousness, truth and *Dharma*.

Chapter VII

ॐ

Ethics of Vidura.
Sanskrit Shlokas:

1. निषेवते प्रशस्तानि निन्दितानि न सेवते ।
   अनास्तिकः श्रद्दधान एतत् पण्डितलक्षणम् ॥

2. क्रोधो हर्षश्च दर्पश्च हीर्दभ्भो मान्यमानिता ।
   यमर्थान्नापकर्षन्ति स वै पण्डित उच्यते ॥

3. यस्य कृत्ये न विघ्नति शीतमुष्णं भयं रतिः ।
   समृद्धिरसमृद्धिर्वा स वै पण्डित उच्यते ॥

4. क्षिप्रं विजानाति चिरं शृणोति ।
   विज्ञाय चार्थं भजते न कामत् ।
   नासंपृष्टो ह्युपपुङ्क्ते परार्थे ।
   तत् प्रज्ञानं प्रथमं पण्डितस्य ॥

5. नाप्राप्यमभिवाञ्छन्ति नष्टं नेच्छन्ति शोचितुम् ।
   आपतसु च न मुह्यन्ति नराः पण्डितबुद्धयः ॥

6. आर्यकर्मणि रज्यन्ते भूतिकर्माणि कुर्वते ।
   हितं च नाभ्यसूयन्ति पण्डिता भरतर्षभ ॥

7. तत्त्वज्ञः सर्वभूतानां योगज्ञः सर्वकर्मणां ।
   उपायज्ञो मनुष्याणां नरः पण्डित उच्यते ॥

8. स्वमर्थे यः परित्यज्य पर्थमबुतिष्ठते ।
   मिथ्या चरते मित्रार्थे यश्च मूढः स उच्यते ॥

9. अनाहूतः प्रविशति ह्यपृष्टो बहु भाषते ।
   अविश्वस्ते विश्वसिति मूढचेता नराधमः ॥

10. अर्थे महान्तमासद्य विद्यामैश्वर्यमेव वा ।
विचरत्यसमुन्नद्धो य: स पण्डित उच्यते ॥

11. एक: समान्नमश्रति वस्ते वासश्च शोभनम् ।
योऽसंविभज्य भृत्येभ्य: को नृशंसतरस्तत: ॥

12. एकं हन्यात्र वा हन्यादिपुरुमुक्तो धनुष्माता ।
बुद्धिर्बुद्धिमतोत्सृष्टा हन्याद्राष्ट्रं सराजकम् ॥

13. सत्यं स्वर्गस्य सोपानं पारावारस्य नौरिव ।

14. एक: क्षेमवतां दोष: द्वितीयो नापपद्यते ।
यदेनं क्षमया युक्तमशक्तं मन्यते जन: ॥

15. सोऽस्य दोषो न मन्तव्य: क्षमा हि परमं वचम् ।
क्षमा गुणो हि अशक्तानां शक्तानां भूषणं क्षमा ॥

16. क्षमा वशीकृतिर्लोके क्षमया किं न साध्यते ।
शान्तिखड्गं करे यस्य दुर्जन: किं करिष्यति ॥

17. एको धर्म: परं श्रेय: क्षमया किं न साध्यते ।
विद्यैका परमा तृप्तिरहिंसैका सुखावहा ॥

18. त्रिविधं नरकस्येदं द्वारं नाशनमात्मन: ।
काम: क्रोधस्तथा लोभस्तस्मादेतत्त्रयं ज्यजेत् ॥

19. षड्दोषा पुरुषेणेह हातव्या भूतिमिच्छता ।
निद्रा तन्द्रा भयं क्रोध आलस्यं दीर्घमृत्रिता ॥

20. दर्भ मोह मत्सरं पापकृत्यं राजोद्दिष्टं पैशुनं पूगवैरं ।
मत्तोन्मत्तैर्दुर्धनैश्चापि वादो य: प्रज्ञावान् वर्जयेत् स प्रधान: ।

21. मितं भुङ्क्ते संविभज्याश्रितेभ्यो
मितं स्वपिति मितं कर्म कृत्वा
ददात्यमित्रेष्वपि याचित: सन् ।
तमात्मवन्तं प्रनहत्यनर्था: ॥

22. यच्छक्यं ग्रासेतुं ग्रस्यं ग्रस्तं परिणमेच्च यत् ।
हितं च परिणामे यत्तदाद्यं भूतिमिच्छता ।

23. सत्येन रक्ष्यते धर्मो विद्या रोगेन रक्ष्यते ।
मज्ज्या रक्ष्यते रूपं कुलं वृत्तेन रक्ष्यते ॥

24. न कुलं वृत्तहीनस्य प्रमाणमिति मे मति: ।
अप्त्यष्वेपि हि जातानां वृत्तमेव विशिष्यते ॥

25. विद्यामदो धनमदस्तृतीयोऽभिजने मद: ।
मदा ह्येतेऽवलिप्तानां एत एव सतां दमा: ॥

26. शीलं प्रधानं पुरुषे तदस्येह प्रणस्यति ।
    न तस्य जीवितेनार्थो न धनेन न बन्धुभिः ॥

27. अवृत्तिर्भयमन्त्यानां मध्यानां मरणाद्भयम् ।
    उत्तमानां तु मर्त्यानामवमानात् परं भयम् ॥

28. रोहते सायकैर्विद्धं वनं परशुनाऽऽहतम् ।
    वाचा दुरुक्तं बीभत्सं न प्ररोहति वाक्क्षतम् ।

29. यथा यथा हि पुरुषः कल्याणे कुरुते मनः ।
    तथा तथास्य सर्वार्थाः सिध्यन्ते नात्र संशयः ॥

30. मद्यपानं कलहं पूगवैरं भार्यापत्योरन्तरं ज्ञातिभेदम् ।
    राजाद्विष्टं स्त्रीपुंसयोर्विवादं वर्ज्यान्याहुः:–

31. जरा रूपं हरति हि धैर्यमाशा ।
    मृत्यु प्राणाम् धर्मचर्यामसूया ॥

32. अष्टो गुणः पुरुषं दीपयन्ति प्रज्ञा च कौल्यं च दमश्रुतं च ।
    पराक्रमश्चबहुभाषिता च दानं यथाशक्ति कृतज्ञता च ॥

33. इज्याध्ययनदानानि तपः सतये क्षमा घृणा ।
    अलोभ इति मार्गोऽयं धर्मस्याष्टविधः स्मृत ॥

34. पूर्वे वयसि तत्कुर्याद्येन वृद्धः सुखं वसेत् ।
    यावज्जीवेन तत्कुर्याद्धिन प्रेत्य सुखं वसेत् ॥

35. यादृशैः सह विसन्ति यादृशांश्चोपसेवते ।
    यादृगिच्छेत् भवितुं तादृग्भवति पूरुषः ॥

36. भावमिच्छति सर्वस्य नाभावो कुरुते मनः ।
    मत्यवादी मृदुर्दान्तो यः स उत्तमपूरुषः ॥

37. सुखं च दुःखं च भावाभावौ च लाभालाभौ मरणं जीवितं च ।
    पर्यायशः सर्वमेतं स्पृशन्ति तस्माद्धीरो न प्रहृष्येत्र शोचित ॥

38. सुलभाः पुरुषा राजन् सततं प्रियवादिनः ।
    अप्रियस्य च पथ्यस्य वक्ता श्रोता च दुर्लभः ॥

39. गुणा दश स्नानशीलं भजन्ते बलं रूपं स्वरवर्णप्रशुद्धिः ।
    स्पर्शश्च गन्धश्च विशुद्धता च श्रीः सौकुमार्ये प्रवराश्च नार्यः ॥

40. गुणाश्च षण्मितभुक्तं भजन्ते आरोग्यमायुश्च बलं सुखं च ।
    अनाविलं चास्य भवत्यपत्यं न चैनमाद्यून इति क्षिपन्ति ॥

41. वृद्धिः प्रभावस्तेजश्च सत्त्वमुत्थानमेव च ।
    व्यवसायश्च यस्य स्यात्तस्याऽवृत्तिभयं कुतः ॥

42. कर्माणां तु प्रशस्तानां अनुष्ठनं सुखावहम् ।
    तेषामेवाननुष्ठानं पश्चात्तापकरं मतम् ॥

43. दैवतेषु प्रयत्नेन राजसु ब्राह्मणेषु च ।
    नियन्तव्य: सदा क्रोधो वृद्धबालातुरेषु च ॥

44. कर्मणा मनसा वाचा यदभीक्ष्णं निषेवते ।
    तदेवापहरत्येनं तस्मात् कल्याणमाचारेत् ॥

45. नित्यो धर्म: सुखदु:खेत्वनित्ये जीवो नित्यो हेतुरस्य तवनित्य: ।
    त्यक्त्वाऽनित्यं प्रतितिष्ठस्व नित्यं सन्तुप्य सन्तोष्परो हि लाभ: ॥

46. आत्मा नदी भरत पुण्यतीर्थं सत्योदका धृतिकुला दयोर्मि ।
    तस्या स्नात: पूयते पुण्यकर्मो पुण्यो ह्रात्मा नितयमलोभ एव ॥

Chapter VIII

Ethics of Canakya

꧁

Canakya Niti is a very valuable treatise on political science. The author has dealt with the subject in an admirable manner. Though the central idea in the book treats of the duties of kings, their ministers and other officers of the State, doctrines of ethics too have been explained. Cānakya, the great politician, did realise the significance which a ruler ought to attach to morality and hence it is that he lays down many rules for the guidance even of a lay man. The numbers of the *shlokas* given below refer to the chapters of *'Canakya Niti Darpana'*. Tradition and folklore describe Cānakya to be an officer at the court of Candragupta. In his style there is perspicuity, variety, vigour and simplicity. Here follow some of his *shlokas*.

1. Save wealth as a provision for needy times. There is no knowing when a rich man too will have to feel the pinch of penury.

    Ch. 1. 7.

2. It is not advisible that one should live in a country where the following do not exist:–
    (a) Respectful and hospitable treatment, (b) Means of decent livelihood, (c) Friends and relations, (d) Means of acquiring

knowledge, (e) Rich men prone to give, (f) Wise men. (g) Settled Government, (h) Good water and (i) A competent doctor.

Ch. 1. 8, 9.

3. The worth of a servant is to be tested by sending him on any business, sympathy of relations can be recognised in times of trouble, friends can be tried in one's adversity and wife's love can be realised when poverty overtakes the husband.

Ch. 1. 11.

4. To one having an obedient son and a faithful wife and leading a contented and simple life, even in opulent circumstances this earth is heaven itself.

Ch. 2. 3.

5. Never place confidence in a foe pretending to be a friend. Care should be taken even in confiding your secrets to a friend. Because there is the danger of that friend revealing all your secrets in case he should become displeased with you for some reason or other.

Ch. 2. 6.

6. Those parents who do not educate their children are their enemies, such children are never honoured by wise men.

Ch. 2. 1 I.

7. An uneducated man with all his wealth, beauty, and birth in a noble family is never honoured. He is like a flower without smell.

Ch. 3. 8.

8. Poverty can be warded off by industry. There is no likelihood of a genuine ascetic committing sin. Silence is golden, it gives rise to no quarrel. A cautious man has no cause for fear.

Ch. 3. 11.

9. As long as this body is healthy and death is to occur only after a long time, do good deeds. Decrepitude disables man from doing anything.

Ch. 4. 4

10. Care should always be taken to find out proper time, proper friends, profit and loss in any undertaking and the exact measure of one's abilities.

Ch. 4. 18.

11. Gold is to be tested in four ways, by rubbing it upon a touch-stone, by breaking, by heating and by hammering. Man's worth also can be ascertained by his charity, character, behaviour and actions.

Ch. 5. 2.

12. One ought not to be afraid of a danger till it actually befalls. Having once fallen into it, attempts must be boldly made to get out of the difficulties.

Ch. 5. 3.

13. There is no disease worse than evil passion, no enemy worse than ignorance, no fire like anger and no happiness better than the acquisition of knowledge.

Ch. 5. 12.

14. Wealth and life are transitory. In this ephemeral world virtue alone is permanent.

Ch. 5. 21.

15. An only son endowed with education and virtue becomes the cause of delight to the family, after the manner of the moon to the night.

Ch. 3. 16.

16. These five are to be considered as worthy of respects as the father, (1) Father, (2) Spiritual initiator, (3) Teacher, (4) Giver of food, (5) Protector from any danger. All these are on an equal footing with the father.

Ch. 5. 22.

17. You may win over a greedy man by giving him money, you may propitiate a fool by going according to his wishes, you may satisfy a proud man by your gentle behaviour but a wise man is pleased only by truthfulness.

Beasts too possess certain qualities which a man can worthily imitate.

18. These four virtues are characteristic of a dog:–
    (1) Ambitious but satisfied with a little.
    (2) Fond of sleep but active or sharp in getting up.
    (3) Faithful service of its master,
    (4) Bold in fighting,

19. An ass possesses these qualities which man can safely imitate:–
    (1) It carries the burden even when it is tired and thus discharges its duty.
    (2) In doing its duty, it is indifferent to the effects of extremes of cold and heat.
    (3) It leads a life of contentment.

A cock rises early and eats whatever it obtains in company with its chickens or friends, while a bird of the crow kind provides itself in time with the necessities for the rainy days and an ant teaches one to be industrious.

Ch. 6. 15, 20.

20. Contentment is a continual feast.

Ch. 7. 3.

21. Flow of water maintains purity in a tank. Such a loss of water is no loss. Similarly wealth spent in discriminate charity is not lost.

Ch. 7. 14.

22. A wise man attains purity of speech and mind and is kind to all sentient beings.

Ch. 7. 20.

23. Know thyself. See the essence of life. Mark you, there is sugar in sugar-cane, ghee in milk and fragrance in a flower.

Ch. 7. 21.

24. If you desire freedom from bondage and perfect happiness, practise forgiveness, pity, purity and truth. Never become, O friend, a slave to passion.

Ch. 9. I.

25. A man is not considered low in spirit because he is not rich. In case he has no education, he is certainly considered mean (Honour depends not upon wealth, but upon knowledge).

Ch. 10. 1.

26. Walk carefully, drink filtered water, speak, sense and do such things as are approved by conscience.

Ch. 10.

27. An earnest student should give up anger, passion, greed, stimulants, love-affairs, too much playful nature, too much sleep and full-time service of any one.

28. Grieve not for the past. Be not overanxious for the future. Think of the present and act after the manner of the wise.

Ch. 14. 20.

29. Keep wicked men at arm's length. Keep company with the noble-minded. Day and night do good deeds. Remember the ephemeral nature of this existence.

30. Let me not acquire that wealth which is obtained by teasing others, by violating the laws of equity, and by crushing enemies.

Ch. 16. 11.

Chapter VIII

ॐ

Ethics of Chanakya.
Sanskrit Ślokas:

1. आपदर्थे धनं रक्षेत् श्रीमतश्च किमापद: ।

2. यस्मिन्देशे न संमानो न वृत्तिर्न च बान्धवा ।
   न च विद्यागमोप्यस्ति वासं तत्र न कारयेत् ॥
   धनिक: श्रेत्रियो राजा नदी वैद्यास्तु पञ्चम: ।
   पञ्च न यह विद्यन्ते न तत्र दिवसं वसेत् ॥

3. जानीयात् प्रेषणे भृत्यान् बान्धवान् व्यसनागमे ।
   मित्रं चापत्तिकाले तु भर्यां च विभवक्षये ॥

4. यस्य पुत्रो वशीभूतो भर्या च्छन्दानुगामिनी ।
   विभवे यश्च सन्तुष्ट: तस्य स्वर्ग इहैव हि ॥

5. न विश्वसेत् कुमित्रे च मित्रेचापि न विश्वसेत् ।
   कदाचित् कुपितं मित्रं सर्वं गुह्यां प्रकाशयेत् ॥

6. माता शत्रु: पिता वैरी येन बालो न पाठित: ।
   न शोभते सभामध्ये हंसमध्ये बको यथा ॥

7. रूपयौवनसंपन्ना विशालकुलसंभवा ।
   विद्याहीना न शोभन्ते निर्गन्धा इव किंशूका: ॥

8. उद्योगे नास्ति दारिद्रयं जपतो नास्ति पातकम् ।
   मौने च कलहो नास्ति नास्ति जागरिते भयम् ॥

9. यावतस्वस्थो ह्ययं देहो यावन्मृत्युश्च दूरत: ।
   तावदात्महितं कुर्यात् प्राणान्ते किं करिष्यति ॥

10. क: काल: कानि मित्राणि को देश: को व्ययागमौ ।
    कस्याहं का च मे शक्ति: इति चिन्तयं मुहुर्मुह: ॥

11. यथा चतुर्भिः कनकं परीक्ष्यते निघर्षणच्छेदनतापताडनैः ।
    तथा चतुर्भिः पुरुषः परीक्ष्यते त्यागेन दानेन गुणेन कर्मणा ॥

12. तावद्भयेषु भेतव्यं । यावद्भयं नागतम् ।
    आगतं तु भयं दृष्ट्वा प्रहर्त्तव्यमशङ्कया ॥

13. नास्ति कामसमो व्याधिर्नास्ति मोहसमो रिपुः ।
    नास्ति कोपसमो वह्निः नास्ति ज्ञानसमं सुखम् ॥

14. चला लक्ष्मीश्चलाः प्राणाश्चले जीवितमन्दिरे ।
    चलाचले च संसारे धर्म एकोहि निश्चलः ॥

15. एकेनापि सुपुत्रेण विद्यायुक्तेन साधुना ।
    आह्लादितं कुलं सर्वं यथा चन्द्रेण शर्वरी ॥

16. जनिता चोपनेता च यस्तु विद्यां प्रयच्छति ।
    अन्नदाता भवत्राता पञ्चैते पितरः स्मृताः ॥

17. लुब्धमर्थेन गृह्णीयात् स्तब्धमञ्जलिकर्मणा ।
    मूर्खं छन्दानुवृत्त्या च यथार्थत्वेन पण्डितम् ॥

18. बह्वशीस्वल्पसन्तुष्टः सुनिद्रः शीघ्रचेतनः ।
    सन्तुष्टश्चरते नित्यं त्रीणि शिक्षेच्चगर्दभात् ॥

19. सुश्रान्तोऽपि वहेद्भारं शीतोष्णे न पश्यति ।
    सन्तुष्टश्चरते शश्च षडेते श्वानतो गुणाः ॥

20. सन्तोषामृततृप्तानां सुखं शान्तिरेव च ।

21. उपार्जितानां वित्तानां त्याग एव हि रक्षणम् ।
    तडागोदरसंस्थानां परिस्रव इवाम्भसाम् ॥

22. वाचा शौचं च मनसः परार्थिनाम् ।

23. पुष्पे गन्धं तिले तैलं काष्ठेऽग्निं पयसि घृतम् ।
    इक्षौ गुडं तथा देहे पश्यात्मानं विवेकतः ॥

24. मुक्तिमिच्छमि चेत् तात विषयान् विषवत् व्यज ।
    क्षमार्जवदयाशौचं सत्यं पीयूषवत् पिब ॥

25. धनहीनो न हीनश्च धनिकः स सुनिश्चयः ।
    विद्यारत्नेन यो हीनः स हीनः सर्ववस्तुषु ॥

26. दृष्टिपूतं न्यसेत् पादं वस्त्रपूतं जलं पिबेत् ।
    शास्त्रपूतं वदेद्वाक्यं मनः पूतं समाचरेत् ॥

27. कामक्रोधौ तथा लोभं स्वादु शृङ्गारकौतुके ।
    अतिनिद्रातिसेवे च विद्यार्थी ह्यष्टवर्जयेत् ॥

28. गते शोको न कर्तव्यो भविष्यंनेव चिन्तयन् ।
वर्तमानेन कालेन प्रवर्तन्ते विचलक्षण: ॥

29. व्यज दुर्जनसंसर्गं भज साधुसमागमम् ।
कुरु पुण्यं अहोरात्रं स्मर नित्यमनितयताम् ॥

30. अतिक्लेशेन ये अर्था धर्मस्यातिक्रमेण तु ।
शत्रूणां प्राणिपातेन अर्था मा भवन्तु मे ॥

Chapter IX

Ethics of Shukráchárya

࿇

A mong the many NITI-SHASTRAS extant in Sanskrit literature, SHUKRA-NITI occupies a place of honour. This work is an excellent treatise on ethics, state-craft, sociology, mineralogy and geography and as such, it deserves wide reading and careful study. Its style is, indeed, antique and charming and reminds one of the times of Válmiki and Vyása. The very-arrangement of the SHLOKAS is characteristic of the classic period in Sanskrit literature. Some of the critics, however, are inclined to believe that the work is of a recent date and at the most, a collection of a few fabricated verses. A student of history with a critical bent of mind, receives a surprising shock, when he finds guns, cannons, clocks, and gunpowder and its manufacture, mentioned in this NITI. It must, nevertheless, be admitted that the fixing of an accurate date of the author, either from internal, or external evidence is a pretty difficult task. Tradition and folklore describe him as the priest and preceptor of the ASURAS. An element of truth seems to lurk in this tradition. In the historic development of the early Aryan race, the ASURAS and the SURAS occupy the position of two opposite poles. While the SURAS considered life on this earth a mere dream and an illusion, the ASURAS thought it was real and full of meaning. The character manifested by the DEVATAS was one of a meditative and a passive nature, while the ASURAS revealed one of a militant and aggressive type. The ASURAS dedicated their lives to the worship of matter, while the SURAS sacrificed their all, in the service of spirit. These DAITYAS were always bent upon making conquests after conquests of new lands and building and planning new cities and formidable forts, while the DEVATAS led a holy, pious, and peaceful life, and were subjected to many acts of tyranny by the RAKSHASAS. We consequently hear of DEVASURA-SANGRAMA in Sanskrit literature. It is but natural, therefore, to expect that the priest and preceptor of such a mighty race should compose a book for the guidance of his pupil-race. Treating as it does of a multitude of subjects of varying degrees of importance, this Niti is of a cyclopædic nature. The principles of ethics and state-craft enunciated therein are well-calculated to exert a healthy influence on those for whom the Niti was primarily meant, as well as on those, who are of an ASURIC nature, even in modern times. The ASURAS, however, seem never to have digested the wise sayings of their GURU and naturally, they met with the inevitable downfall, so much so, to the present day, there is hardly any monument of their greatness left by them, to tell to future ages, the doleful story of their rapid rise and quicker downfall. In their zeal and enthusiasm for acquiring lands, they never cared to approach the ideals of kingship presented by their Guru, and in their rule of subject-races they rode rough-shod over their feelings. They ruled with an iron-rod. Sympathy never formed the keynote of their policy. They ingeniously eliminated the rules of equity from their tyrannical rule, and the gulf between the rulers and the ruled was gradually widened and it was not even in the power of SHUKRACHARYA to bridge it over. In due course, they were driven to the rock of ruin by their own folly and arrogance. Rulers like Ahi, Mahi, HIRANYAKSHA and HIRANYA-KASHYAPA, and RAKSHASAS, like RAVANA and KANSA fell victims to such a treacherous policy. Powerful kings like BALI were crumbled to dust simply because their civilisation, of whatever type it was, was never founded on ethics, equity and benevolence. Here follow a few shlokas from SHUKRANITI, treating of the rules of conduct.

1. There can be no happiness without virtue. Follow, therefore, the path of righteousness.

   Ch. III. 2.

2. Give up murder, theft, slander, cruelty, deceit, creating discontent, and inimical feelings.

   Ch. III. 7.

3. There are sins likely to be committed by mind, body and speech. Give them up entirely. Protect the poor, the sick, and the distressed, as far as your circumstances permit.

   Ch. III. 8.

4. Consider the life even of an ant or any insect as sacred as your own life. Be guided by feelings of philanthropy even towards your enemies.

   Ch. III. 9.

5. Do not subject you senses to too much severity, nor do you become a slave of them. (Neither be a Stoic nor an Epicurean.)

   Ch. XIV. 1.

6. Man, desirous of attaining prosperity should give up excessive sleep, idleness, fear, anger and dilatoriness.

   Ch. III. 53.

7. Be constantly engaged in the discharge of your legitimate duties....Speak gentle words.

8. Do not divulge your domestic secrets, unless there be a special occasion for it. Speak little, but only sense.

   Ch.III. 59.

9. Admire virtues even if they be found in your enemies but abandon those vices even though they be found in your own tutor.

Ch. III. 65.

10. Have foresight and presence of mind. After the undertaking of a work, be neither hasty nor dilatory.

Ch. III. 67.

11. Honour those that deserve it. A king ought not to inflict cruel punishment and utter harsh words.

Ch. III. 81.

12. Listen always attentively to the glorious deeds of philanthropists, donors and brave men. Attach no importance to their flaws.

Ch. III. 106.

13. Never treat the blind, the deaf and the cripple with contempt.

Ch. III. 111.

14. Never disobey the commands of the king, and of the noble-minded persons.

Ch. IIII. 11.

In the 126th *shloka* he describes the advantages of travel.

15. Travel acquaints a man with the conditions, customs and manners of different peoples. A traveller can also see how a king dispenses justice elsewhere and realise what history is and what constitutes dishonesty.

Ch. III. 127.

16. Avoid the company of suspicious characters. Never listen to the private conversation of others.

Ch. III. 139.

17. Thinking that death is approaching you soon and the period of life is short, try your best to do good and virtuous acts.

Ch. III. 200.

18. Discharge of one's own duty gives greatest happiness and by itself is the great TAPAS.
19. AHIMSA (love of life—not killing any living object) is a great DHARMA. (Cf. Patanjali's Yoga Darshana)

Ch. I. 58.

In the fourth chapter there is the description of ITHIHASA, PURANAS, the VEDAS and their Angas. The first chapter pre-eminently treats of the duties of kings, and in many other SHLOKAS, there are plans of building cities and palaces and frequent references are made to council meetings and the duties of citizens in general. The book, on the whole, is a mine of information, on varied subjects and enables one to determine the high watermark of the type of civilisation of those times.

Chapter IX

ॐ

Ethics of Shukracharya.
Sanskrit Ślokas:

1. सुखंच नविनाधर्मात्तस्माद्धर्मपरो भवेत् ।
2. हिंसास्तेयान्यथा कामं पैशून्यं परुषानृतम् ॥
   संभिन्नालापव्यापादमभिध्यादृग्विपर्ययम् ॥
3. पाकर्मेतिदशधाकायवाङ्मानसैः तयजेत् ।
   अवृत्तिव्याधिशोकातनि अनुवर्तेत शक्तितः ॥
4. आत्मवत् सततं पश्येदपि कीटापेपीलिकम् ।
   उपकारः प्रधानस्यादपकारपरेष्वरौ ॥
5. न पीडयोदिन्द्रियाणि न चैतान्यतिलालयेत् ॥
6. षड्दोषा पुरुषेणेह हातब्या भूतिमिच्छता ।
   निद्रा तंद्रा भयं क्रोध अलस्यं दीर्घमृत्रता ॥
7. स्वधर्मनिरतो नित्यं परस्त्रीषु पराङ्मुखः ।
   वक्तो हवाँश्चित्रकथः स्यादकुढित वाक्सदा ॥
8. अपृष्टौ नैव कथरायेदृहकृत्य तु कं प्रति ।
   बह्वथाल्पाक्षरं कुर्यात्संल्लापं कार्यसाधकम् ॥
9. शत्रोरपि गुणग्राह्या गुरोस्त्याज्यास्तु दुर्गुणम् ।
10. दीर्घदर्शी सदा च स्यात् प्रत्युत्पन्नमतिः क्वचित् ।
    साहसी सालसी चैव चिरकारी भवेन्नाही ॥
11. दानैर्मानैश्च सतकारैः सुपूज्यान् पूजयेत् सदा ।
    कदापि नोगदण्डः स्यात् कटुभाषणतत्परः ॥

12. दातॄणां धार्मिकाणां च शूराणां कीर्तनं सदा ।
शृणुयात्तु प्रयत्नेन तच्छिद्रं नवलक्षयेत् ॥

13. दीनांधपंगुबधिरा नोपहास्या: कदाचन ।

14. आज्ञाभङ्गस्तु महतां राज्ञ: कार्यो नवै क्वचित् ।

15. देशाटनात् स्वानुभूता: पर्वतादेशरीतय: ।
कीदृशा राजपुरुषा न्याय्यन्याय्यं च कीदृशम् ॥

16. संशकितानां समीप्यं तयजेद् वै नीचसेवनम् ।
यंत्रापं नैव शृणुयाद् गुप्त: कस्यापि सर्वदा ॥

17. स्थितो मृत्युमुखे चाहं क्षणमायुर्ममास्ति न ।
इति मत्वा दानधर्मौ यथेष्टौ च समाचरेत् ।

18. विना स्वधर्मात्र सुखं स्वधर्मोतु परंतप: ।

19. आनृशंस्यं परो धर्म: सर्वप्राणाभृतान् यत: ।

Chapter X

Ethics of the Bhagavad-Gita

Of the many ethical gems found in Sanskrit literature, the Bhagavadgītā is the brightest. In all ages and climes, it is bound to shed lustre and lead man on to that goal towards which perfected humanity is marching. Its message is one of peace, love, and harmony. It has preached in immortal strains that, under all circumstances, happy or miserable, man has to discharge the duty entrusted to him, in the worthiest possible manner. Irrespective of the consequences man is to think of doing good. Virtuous life must be led not because it gives happiness, but because of virtue alone. Virtue for virtue's sake is its teaching. Duty for duty's sake is its refrain. In the midst of worldly cares and anxieties, at a time when sorrows, miseries and sad disappointments overtake us, that we are not to lose heart but we ought to try our utmost to maintain equilibrium and manfully fight with them, is its burden. In this KURUKSHETRA of SAMSARA—worldly existence—temptations in the form of Kauravas deceive man, the Arjuna, and render him impotent, weak and imbecile, and then it is that Krishna—Superior form of *Knowledge* and *Bhakti*—exhorts him to be manly, brave and courageous and to discharge his duties, however unpleasant they may seem to us, outsiders.

Mrs Annie Besant has rightly observed that 'the Bhagavadgītā is a true scripture of the Race, a life, rather than a book. For each age, it has a new message, for each civilisation a new word. Once, it said to India "Meditate;" and she meditated so long that her meditation has passed into drowsiness. Now, it cries to India "Act," and the call is echoing through the land, awakening everywhere a longing for action. But action to be useful must be wise; action to be useful must aim at the common good and must be the harmonious working out of the *Supreme Will.'* (Introduction to Mr F.T. Brook's *Gospel of Life*). Herein lies the ethical significance of this immortal *'Lord's Song'*. It is idle to think that the teachings of the Gita are merely speculative. They have a direct bearing on the practical concerns of life, in any age and in any clime.

Sir Edwin Arnold records:–

'In plain but noble language, it unfolds a philosophical system which remains to this day the prevailing Brahmanical belief, blending as it does the doctrines of Kapila, Patanjali, and the Vedas. So lofty are many of its declarations, so sublime its aspirations, so tender and pure its piety, that Schlegel, after his study of the poem, breaks forth into an outburst of delight and praise towards its unknown author.'

Lassen re-echoes this splendid tribute and says:–

'Indeed so striking are some of the moralities here inculcated and so close the parallelism—at a time actually verbal—between its teachings and those of the New Testament that a controversy has arisen between Pandits and Missionaries on the point whether the author borrowed from Christian sources or the Evangelists and Apostles from him.'

Mr V.J. Kirtikar has admirably summed up the whole ethics of the Gitā thus:--

1. Forbear injuring any being.
2. Treat all alike.
3. Help the needy, even at a sacrifice to yourself.
4. Do all your duties in a disinterested spirit and as an offering of love to the Supreme Being in purity of heart.
5. Renounce things earthly, so that your thoughts and deeds might be free from the sting of egotism and also free from earthly desires and attachments, which arouse bad passions and lead one astray.

Here follow a few shlokas in support of these statements:--

1. कुलक्षये प्रणश्यन्ति कुलधर्माः सनातनाः ।
   धर्मे नष्टे कुलं कृत्स्नमधर्मोऽभिभवत्युत ॥

   When a family is destroyed the immemorial DHARMA of the family is destroyed too. The result is that lawlessness prevails everywhere.

2. When Arjuna shrinks from doing his duty, Krishna exhorts him and says—

   क्लैब्यं मास्मगमः पार्थ नैतत्वय्युपपद्यते ।

   Shake off this weakness. Stand up boldly.

3. अशोच्यानान्वशोचस्त्वं प्रज्ञावादांश्च भाषसे ।
   गतासूनगतासूंश्च नानुशोचन्ति पण्डिताः ॥

   You grieve for those that should not be grieved for. . . . Wise men do not grieve, either for the living or for the dead.
   Krishna then emphasises the fact that human soul is imperishable, and men should not allow themselves to be influenced either by pain or by pleasure, in the discharge of their legitimate duties. They should try and maintain equanimity of temper and not be swayed by sorrow.

4. अव्यवसायिनां बुद्धयो बहु शाखा ह्यनन्ताश्च ॥

Irresolute men entertain endless thoughts and do not do any definite work.

Ch. II. 41.

5. कर्मण्येवाधिकारस्ते मा फलेषु कदाचन ।
   मा कर्मफलहेतुर्भूर्मा ते सङ्गोऽस्त्वकर्मणि ॥

Think mainly of the action. Do not neglect the same, being in doubt of its results. The fruit of action should not be the guiding principles nor should one be attached to inaction.

Ch. II. 47.

6. दुःखेष्वनुद्विग्नमनाः सुखेषु विगतस्पृहः ।
   वीतरागभयक्रोधः स्थितधीर्मुनिरुच्यते ॥

The mind of that sage is said to be stable, when it is not cowed down by anxiety and is not overjoyed in pleasure, and when it is free from anger and passion.

Ch. II. 59.

7. क्रोधाद्भवति संमोहः संमोहात् स्मृतिविभ्रमः ।
   स्मृतिभ्रंशाद्बुद्धिनाशोबुद्धिनाशात् प्रणश्यति ॥

Anger gives rise to delusion and delusion weakens the memory. Weakness of memory leads on to the destruction of the discriminating power and from this intellect and reasoning faculties are lost. Avoid, therefore, anger.

Ch. III. 63.

8. न कर्मणामनारम्भनौष्कर्म्यं पुरुषोऽश्नुते ।
   न च संन्यसनादेव सिद्धिं समधिगच्छति ॥

Inactivity is not freedom. Renunciation leads not to perfection [Philosophy of quietism is condemned here].

Ch. III. 4.

9. श्रेयान्स्वधर्मो विगुण: परधर्मात्स्वनुष्ठितात् ।
   स्वधर्मो निधनं श्रेय: परधर्मो भयावह: ॥

The performance of one's own duty is better though it may appear to others as wanting in merit, than that of another. Death, in the discharge of one's own duty, is preferable. Other's duty is full of danger.

Ch. IV. 35.

10. न हि ज्ञानेन सदृशं पवित्रमिह विद्यते ।

There is nothing holier than wisdom [Acquire it].

Ch. IV. 38.

11. ज्ञानं लब्ध्वा परां शान्तिमचिरेणाधिगच्छति ।

Having obtained wisdom man soon acquires peace of mind.

12. विद्याविनयसंपन्ने ब्राह्मणे गवि हस्तिनि ।
    शुनि चैव श्वपाके च पण्डिता: समदर्शिन: ॥

Wise men consider that all are equal. They make no difference in their attachment towards any, whether learned or the lowest born. The intelligent and the ignorant, the high-born or the low-born are the same to them.

Ch. V. 18.

13. अद्वेष्टा सर्वभूतानां मैत्र: करुण एव च ।
    निर्ममो निरहंकार: समदु:खसुख: क्षमी ॥

He is the beloved of God, who is free from ill-will towards any being, is friendly and sympathetic, has no pride, maintains equilibrium of mind either in pain or in pleasure, and who is contented and resolute in will.

In the succeeding SHLOKAS it is declared that men who are pure in nature, who treat friends or foes alike, and who are unaffected, either by praise or censure, are also liked by God.

14. The following are some of the virtues recommended to be practised:–
(1) Humility, (2) Unpretentiousness, (3) Harmlessness, (4) Forgiveness, (5) Straightforwardness, (6) Service to a teacher, (7) Purity of body and mind, (8) Steadfastness, (9) Control of the senses.

अमानित्वं अदम्भित्वं अहिंसाक्षान्तिरार्जवम् ।
आचार्योपासनं शौचं स्थैर्यमात्मविनिग्रहः ॥

15. Why should not a man destroy anything ?
It is because that the same Guiding Power is present everywhere and this principle is recognised by a wise man.

समं पश्यन्त्रहि सर्वत्र समवस्थितमीश्वरम ।
नहिनस्त्यात्मनात्मानं ततो यांति परां गतिम् ॥

In the XIVth chapter there is the description of the three GUNAS and their characteristics. Great importance is attached to the development of SATTVIKA nature.

16. कर्मणः सुकृतस्याहुः सात्विकं निर्मलं फलम् ।
रजसस्तु फलं दुःखमज्ञानं तमसः फलम् ॥

Mental harmony is the result of SATTVIKA nature, misery that of RAJASIKA and ignorance that of TAMASIK nature.

Ch. XIV., 10.

17. He who is above these GUNAS is described as one, who is the same in honour and dishonour, and is not deeply absorbed in undertakings alone.

Ch. XIV., 25.

In the xvth Discourse, there is the description of that happy abode to which the following are said to reach—

18. निमीनमोहा जितसङ्गदोषा: ।
    अध्यात्मनित्या विनिवृत्तकामा: ॥
    द्वन्द्वैर्विमुक्ता: सुखद   :खसंज्ञै ।
    गच्छन्त्यमूढा: पदमव्ययं तत् ॥

Those wise men who are free from egotism, who have triumphed over attachment, who are constantly thinking of that Great Self and who are unaffected either by pain or pleasure, attain that blissful state.

Ch. XV., 5.

The ethical system advocated in the XVIth, XVIIth and XVIIIth chapters seems to re-echo the sentiments expressed in the UPANISHADS and the MANU SMRITI. In the first few verses of the XVIth Discourse the following virtues are dilated and commented upon—

(1) अभय = Fearlessness, (2) सत्त्वसंशुद्धि = Purity of body and mind, (3) दानं = Charity, (4) अहिंसा = Harmlessness, (5) सत्यं = Truth, (6) धृति: = Courage, (7) मार्दवं = Gentleness.

There is also a classification known as ĀSURIKA and DAIVIKA types of men (Good and Bad). Among the former are included the atheists, men of aggressive and quarrelsome nature, men proud of their wealth and position in life and those that cast the scriptures to the winds.

In the XVIIth Discourse there is the threefold division of men according to their nature—SATTVIKA, RAJASIKA and TAMASIKA. There are three verses, which show that even the nature of the food these partake is different. Men of the highest (SATTVIKA) type take such food as is delicious, agreeable and energy-giving, while to the second (RAJASIKA), it is said, that they like bitter, sour and pungent things, and the last (TAMASIKA) prefer stale, putrid and unclean things.

Ch. XVII. 8, 9 & 10.

Similar classification is made of charity and penance also. The SATTVIKA DANA—the noblest form of charity—is that, which is given without expecting anything in return and which is considerate, regarding time and place and person. That charity is of the RAJASIKA nature, which is given not for charity's sake, but for receiving some benefit out of it. That which is given not caring for time or place, and given to undeserving persons and sometimes out of contempt, and wrath too, is of the worst type.

Ch. XVII, 20, 21 & 22.

Ultimately man is advised to lead a virtuous life, free from pride, egotism, cruelty and wickedness, and to discharge his legitimate duties, being unmindful of reward or punishment, sorrow or happiness, and thus seek solace, comfort, and happiness, and finally reach that GOAL of all goals.

Of late, profound scholars, keen-witted theologians and enlightened patriots have been vying with one another to expound the GITA according to their own predilections. Year in and year out, commentaries after commentaries and new interpretations after interpretations are being put forward and a layman feels bewildered at this ever-increasing mass of GITA literature. It is THE book which seems to appeal to all kinds of readers. If the dignity of the convocation addresses delivered by the erudite vice-chancellors of Indian Universities is enhanced by constant references to the teachings of Śrī Krishna, the melancholy reflections of a scholar lodged in the solitary cells of a prison-house also are rendered thereby more pathetic. The profound influence which this remarkable book has been all along exercising over the minds of the people drives one to the only conclusion that it is THE standard work on the Hindu Philosophy of Ethics. Mr B.G. Tilak, in his *magnum opus*, the GITA-RAHASYAM, has discussed at great length its ethical significance. In a voluminous work of about a thousand pages of closely printed matter the talented author has instituted a contrast between the teachings of such moral philosophers as Kant, Mill, Spencer and Green and those of Lord Krishna, the great Hindu Philosopher-statesman of the pre-Bhuddistic period of Indian history. The book by itself is a mine of information on such subjects as BHAKTI-YOGA, JNANA-YOGA and KARMA-YOGA. If the theme of the book be compared to a big city with many gates, the author holds that the KARMA-YOGA is its main gate. Philosophy of disinterested action is the burden of the 'Song celestial', and Mr Tilak has laboured hard to bring this aspect of philosophy to the forefront. It should also be noted that this Karma-Yoga is not mere blind action but it is 'JNANA-BHAKTI-YUKTA-KARMA-YOGA'. Without BUDDHI-YOGA, action will degenerate into licentiousness, liberty will mean freedom to do what one likes, and in society chaos will reign supreme. In ancient India, the ASURAS practised it without BUDDHI-YOGA—philosophy of Reason—and BHAKTI-YOGA—philosophy of Love. In our own times, the pre-war Germans also repeated the experiment and the results were in both cases disastrous. Unbridled action leads to recklessness. BUDDHI-YOGA demands control of passions, refinement of intellect and purity of thought and word. BHAKTI-YOGA requires sympathy, fellow-feeling and an earnest desire for the good of mankind. LOKA-SANGRAHA, another great ideal of GITA, presupposes that for harmony and union, for preservation and protection of the people, righteousness is essential. BUDDHI-YOGA and LOKA-SANGRAHA are the pre-requisites of KARMA-YOGA. Action should be sanctified by virtue and it should also be निष्काम, disinterested and unselfish.

For individual happiness the GITA places the ideal of समचित्त्व training of the mind to such a state as to make it unaffected by pleasure or pain. Little worries should not unhinge it and little joys should not elate it. Mental equilibrium both in sorrow and happiness should be maintained. The SAMNYASA-YOGA—the ascetic ideal of renunciation—is not antagonistic to this ideal of action. It has its own place in the history of men and nations. It is an ideal for the few and those few are not entirely valueless. For mystics and saints of the type of Schopenhauer it is the very breath of their nostrils. If that has given them solace and comfort none need condemn the philosophy of Gītā as 'COLD AND LIFELESS.'

In the seventeenth century Saint Ramadāsa of the Maharashtra re-echoed the teachings of Śrī-Krishna and as long as his philosophy guided the Maharatta statesmen, their empire lasted and when it was cast to the winds it inevitably experienced a downfall. When the moral foundations are shaken, no superstructure, however, mighty and grand it may be can afford to stand, The DASA-BODHA of Ramadāsa is practically the Marathi version of the BHAGAVAD-GITA and its lessons, too, are equally sublime and noble. Both these works afford a very interesting and instructive study. Their immediate aims and objects might have been more or less national but their aspirations and ideals are certainly international. They are the products of two masterminds and for every age they have valuable lessons to teach. A diligent student, an astute politician and a stainless saint, nay, a weary traveller on the murky road of life can, one and all, draw inspiration and life-long solace from an impartial study of these two remarkable books.

Chapter XI

Ethics of Bhartrihari

❀

The personal history of Bhartrihari, like the history of almost all the Sanskrit authors, is shrouded in mystery and antiquarians are busy in inventing theories after theories, regarding this author of the three well-known SHATKAS, *viz:*– (1) SHRINGARA-SHATAKA, (2) NITI-SHATAKA and (3) VAIRAGYA-SHATAKA. In all these books, he has recorded his personal experiences based on careful observation of men and manners. In them there is less of speculation and more of common-sense and wisdom. He never soars unusually high on the wings of imagination, dragging the reader, along with him, in the labyrinth of philosophic controversies. He seems to have been bred up in the lap of luxury and fallen a victim to the temptations and miseries of this work-a-day world of ours. But a time must have come in his life, when he must have realised that there was much of folly, ignorance, arrogance, treachery, wickedness and selfishness in this world. This new light, that dawned in him in his riper years, must have enabled him to jot down his actual experiences for the benefit of his fellowmen, as a result of which we have his three SHATAKAS—centuries of couplets—whose condensed style, beautiful similes, vivid description, and sincere exhortations captivate the reader and strongly move him to right actions. His message may be briefly summarised thus:– 'Man, erring man! Be cautious and discreet. Give up mean rivalry and ignoble ambitions. Have no pride of wealth, power or knowledge. Joys of this world are evanescent. Cultivate the virtues of self-sacrifice, philanthrophy, truthfulness and learn to live a higher and nobler life.' This message he has, through his Shatakas, conveyed to the world.

The Shringara-Shataka

The sentiments expressed in this book represent the vigour, vivacity, and buoyancy of youth. There is a graphic description of the nature of woman, of the shafts of love which she darts at man, and of the tangled web which she weaves for him. Man is warned later on to be on his guard.

The Niti-Shataka

From a moral point of view this is supremely an excellent book. The SHLOKAS admirably enlighten our conscience, they preach the equality of man, and vehemently inculcate principles of morality. There is in this a successful 'endeavour to show the difficulty of bringing fools to their senses and the various methods employed by the greedy to acquire wealth.' It is also rich in high sentiments about our conduct in life, such as strictness in adhering to a promise, the value of learning, valour, moral courage and large-mindedness. 'It also inculcates principles which will be met within every religion, the importance of industry, the tests of a true friend, and a contrast of the conduct of a virtuous and noble-hearted man with that of a selfish and narrow-minded individual.' At this stage our author seems to have imbibed VAIRAGYA and composed the next SHATAKA.

The Vairagya-Shataka

In this he has held the greedy to ridicule and the arrogant to contempt. In a forceful style, he points out the high pressure of physical wants felt even by the strongest: he further adds that after all, the joys of the world are of a transient nature and the human beings ought to find consolation in the devotion to the Supreme Being with a view to attain final beatitude.

The immutable and the eternal truths embodied in these couplets will, for all time to come, relieve the distressed, and be like the beaconlight to many a weary sailor, on this stormy ocean of life. They bring peace and goodwill where there are strife, hostility and ill-feelings, and preach morality, without which religion would degenerate into putrified hypocrisy. They preach self-surrender, self-sacrifice, humility, courage, uprightness, love for all sentient beings, and all similar virtues without which no progress, no resuscitation, no true happiness, is possible, whether it be in the case of a single individual or of a society as a whole. The following few SHLOKAS indicate the high watermark of morality, reached in those 'prehistoric' times.

1. Men without a keen intellectual perception suffer a good deal.

2. Those that do not possess education, charitable disposition, amiable nature, good conduct and DHARMA are mere beasts in human form.

Niti. 14.

3. It is better to roam about in dense forests and high mountains in the company of wild beasts, but it is not desirable to be in the company of the wicked, even though it be in the palace of INDRA.

Niti. 16.

4. Neither bracelets nor pearls add to the beauty of man: neither a bath nor the besmearing of the body with SANDAL beautifies the body. Refined speech alone is an ornament.

Niti. 20.

5. Education is an ornament to a man. It is his secret treasure; it gives happiness and fame; it is the preceptor of our preceptors; it is our only friend in a distant land; it alone is respected by kings; and without it, man is no better than a beast.

Niti. 21.

6. If you have forgiveness, you require no other armour; if you have anger, you need not think of a greater enemy; if you have the feeling of brotherhood, nothing can harm you, not even fire; if you have good friends, no other medicine is required; if you are surrounded by wicked men, understand that they are worse enemies than even a poisonous serpent: why should you crave for wealth, if you have education? If you are modest, you stand in need of no other ornament and if you have poetic faculties, even a kingdom will not be of much use to you.

Niti. 12.

7. Those are the noblest of men who are kind to their relatives and strangers, who are ingenious in their dealings with wicked men, who love wise men, who are loyal to their rulers, who honour the learned who are courageous with their enemies, who revere their teachers, and who are shrewd in their dealings with the members of the other sex.

Niti. 23.

8. Good company enlightens us; it makes us lovers of truth; it adds to our honour; it removes our sins; it delights the mind; it spreads our fame far and wide; therefore keep company of the wise and the noble.

Niti. 24.

9. King is ruined by an evil minister; an ascetic by attachment to worldly things; a Brahmin by ignorance; a child by too much fondling; a family by a wicked son; conduct by the company of the wicked; modesty by intoxicating drugs; agriculture by want of proper care; affection by remaining in a distant place without communication of any sort; friendship by mean behaviour; prosperity by extravagance; and wealth by dishonesty.

Niti. 40.

10. Oh, King! This earth is like a cow and the people are like its calf. If you are desirous that she should yield you plenty, take particular care of the people. Rule over them sympathetically.

Niti. 44.

11. Want of sympathy, causeless strife, desire to misappropriate other's wealth, indifference to the welfare of friends and good men—these are some of the characteristics of bad men.

Niti. 50.

12. There is no vice greater than greed; no sin greater than wickedness—(malignant nature); no penance greater than truthful behaviour; purity of mind is the only TIRTHA; good nature is the greatest strength; there is no ornament more beautiful than fame; no wealth equal to knowledge and no death worse than a dishonourable life.

Niti. 53.

13. Life of servitude is indeed miserable; even YOGIS have failed to scrutinise it: if a servant is of a peaceful disposition, he is called dull and stupid: if he talks freely, he is styled a prattler; if he is forgiving, he is known as a coward; and if he does not bear patiently he is supposed to be of ignoble birth.

Niti. 56.

14. That man alone deserves honour who loves the company of the noble, who imitates the virtues of others, who reveres his preceptor, who desires to learn, who loves his own wife,

who is afraid of public censure, who has BHAKTI in God, who has power to control one's senses, and who hates even the contact with the wicked men.

Niti. 60.

15. These are the characteristics of the high-minded:
    1. Firmness in adversity;
    2. Forbearance in prosperity;
    3. Eloquence in an assembly;
    4. Bravery in battle;
    5. Desire for true glory; and,
    6. Devotion to learning.

Niti. 61.

16. A Universal path to happiness is thus described:— Abstinence from destroying life, restraint in depriving others of their wealth, speaking the truth, considerate charity, not even talking of the wives of others, checking the stream of covetousness, reverence for elders, and compassion towards all creatures, these give happiness.

Niti. 63.

(These ideas have made some believe that Bhartrihari was a Buddhist by faith.)

17. If wise men do any act of charity, they keep it a secret: if you go to their houses, you are treated hospitably; they are always silent regarding their good deeds, but are never ashamed to confess their faults, even in an assembly. They are never proud in their opulence and are very cautious in disclosing the defects of others. Who taught the noble to tread in a path which is as difficult as walking on the edge of a sword?

Niti. 66.

The following is a noteworthy division of men:—

18. I call those men best who, not caring for their own good, do good to others; those are mediocres, who do good to others,

but are careful of their own welfare. I consider, however, those as RAKSHASAS—demons—who mar the prospects of others, simply to benefit themselves—but I do not know, by what name to call those that ruin their own cause with a view to ruin others.

Niti. 74.

19. Milk and water are intimate friends. Milk with water was once boiled and naturally water was separated. But milk, being now placed in a miserable plight, thought of falling in that very fire, for the sake of its friend and gradually rose up. But when water was once again added to it, it became pacified. Such is the friendship of good people.

Niti. 76.

(This is one of the most beautiful similes of Bhartrihari).

20. Drive away greed, practice forgiveness, hate that which is evil, speak the truth, tread in the footsteps of great men, serve the learned, honour the noble-minded, treat kindly even those that are your enemies, maintain your reputation and feel compassion for the downtrodden.

Niti. 79.

21. Low-minded men do not undertake any work through fear of meeting with difficulties. Mediocres begin a work but abandon it no sooner obstacles come in their way. But the noble-minded do not give up any work though they meet with any difficulties or failures. They are of a persevering nature while others are not.

Niti. 83.

22. Ambition is in the form of a river, desires are its waters, greed is its waves, passions are its crocodiles, it dashes against the roots of the tree of courage, delusion is its whirlpool, cares and anxieties are its banks. Those wise men who have crossed it are happy.

Vai. 10.

23. In enjoyment there is fear of disease.
    In noble birth there is fear of a fall.
    In wealth there is fear of greedy kings.
    In self-respect there is fear of misery.
    In the body there is fear of death.
    In beauty there is fear of old age.
    In fact every material object is exposed to danger. Only
    VAIRAGYA is free from it.

                                                                Vai. 31.

In many other SHLOKAS Bhartrihari describes that the enjoyments of this world are ephemeral and exhorts men to lead a life of virtue and attain beatitude. These two SHATAKAS are veritable mines of wisdom and valuable maxims applicable to different epochs of life. Undoubtedly Bhartrihari was one of the greatest of Indian ethicists.

Chapter XI

ॐ

Ethics of Bhartrihari.
Sanskrit Shlokas:–

1. विवेकभ्रष्टानां भवति विनिपातः शतमुखः ।
2. येषां न विद्या न तपो न दानं
   ज्ञानं न शीलं न गुणो न धर्मः ।
   ने मर्त्यलोके भुवि भारभूता
   मनुष्यरूपेण मृगाश्चरन्ति ॥
3. वरं पर्वतदुर्गेषु भ्रान्तं वनचरैः सह ।
   न मूर्खजनसंसर्गः सुरेन्द्रभवनेष्वपि ॥
4. केयूरा न विभूष्यन्ति पुरुषं हारा न चन्द्रोज्ज्वला
   न स्नानं न विलेपनं न कुसुमं नालंकृता मूर्धजाः ।
   वाण्येका समलंकरोति पुरुषं या संस्कृता धार्यते
   क्षीयन्तेऽखिलभूषणानि सततं वाग्भूषणं भूषणम् ॥
5. विद्या नाम नरस्य रूपमधिकं प्रच्छन्नगुप्तं धनं
   विद्या भोगकरी यशः सुखकारी विद्या गुरूणां गुरुः ।
   विद्या बन्धुजने विदेशगमने विद्या परा देवता
   विद्या राजसु पूजिता न तु धनं विद्याविहीनः पशुः ॥
6. क्षन्तिश्चेत्कवचेन किं किमरिभिः क्रोधोस्ति चेद्देहिनाम् ।
   ज्ञातिश्चेदनलेन किं यदि सुहृद्दिव्यौषधैः किं फलम् ॥
   किं सर्पैर्यदि दुर्जनाः किमु धनैर्विद्याऽनवद्या यदि ।
   व्रीडा चेत्किमु भूषणैः सुकविता यद्यस्ति राज्येन किम् ॥
7. दाक्षिण्यं स्वजने दया परजने शाक्यं सदा दुर्जने
   प्रीतिः साधुजने नयो नृपजने विद्वज्जनेष्वार्जवम् ।

शौर्यं शत्रुजने क्षमा गुरुजने कान्ताजने धूर्तता
ये चैवं पुरुषाः कलासु कुशलास्तेष्वेव लोकस्थितिः ॥

8. जाड्यं धियो हरति सिञ्चति वाचि सत्यं
मानोन्नतिं दिशति पापमपाकरोति ।
चेतः प्रसादयति दिक्षु तनोति कीर्तिं
सत्सङ्गतिः कथय किं न करोति पुंसाम् ॥

9. दौर्मन्त्र्यान्नृपतिर्विनश्यति यतिः सङ्गात्सुतो लालना
द्विप्रोऽनध्ययननात्कुलं कुतनयाच्छीलं खलोपासनात् ।
ह्रीर्मद्यादनवेक्षणादपि कृषिः स्नेहः प्रवासाश्रयात्
मैत्री चाप्रणयात् समृद्धिरनयात्त्यागात्प्रमादाद्धनम् ॥

10. राजन्दुधुक्षसि यदि क्षितिधेनुमेनां
तेनाद्य वत्समिव लोकममुं पुषाण ।
तस्मिंश्च सम्यगनिशं परिपुष्यमाणे
नानाफलैः फलति कल्पलतेव भूमिः ॥

11. अकरुणत्वमकारणविग्रहः
परधने परयोषिति च स्पृहा ।
सुजनबन्धुजनेष्वसहिष्णुता
प्रकृतिसिद्धमिदं हि दुरात्मनाम् ॥

12. लोभश्चेदगुणेन किं पिशुनता यद्यस्ति किं पातकैः
सत्यं चेत्तपसा च किं शुचि मनो यद्यस्ति तीर्थेन किम ।
सौजन्यं यदि किं बलेन महिमा यद्यारत किं मण्डनैः
सद्विद्या यदि किं धनैरपयशो यद्यस्ति किं मृत्युना ॥

13. मौनान्मूकः प्रवचनपटुश्चाटुलो जल्पको वा
धृष्टः पार्श्वे भवति च वसन् दूरतश्चाप्रगल्भः ।
क्षान्त्या भीरुर्यदि न सहते प्रायशो नाभिजातः
सेवाधर्मः परमगहनो योगिनामप्यगम्यः ॥

14. वाञ्छा सज्जनसङ्गमे परगुणे प्रीतिर्गुरौ नम्रता
विद्यायां व्यसनं स्वयोषिति रतिर्लोकापवादाद्भयम् ।
भक्तिः शूलिनि शक्तिरात्मदमने संसर्गमुक्तिः खलैः
एते येषु वसन्ति निर्मलगुणास्तेभ्यो नरेभ्यो नमः ॥

15. विपदि धैर्यमथाभ्युदये क्षमा
सदसि वाक्पटुता युधि विक्रमः ।
यशसि चाभिरुचिर्व्यसनं श्रुतौ
प्रकृतिसिद्धमिदं हि महात्मनाम् ॥

16. प्राणाघातान्निवृत्ति: परधनहरणे संयम: सत्यवाक्यं
    काले शक्त्या प्रदानं युवतिजनकथामूकभाव: परेषाम् ।
    तृष्णास्रोतोविभङ्गो गुरुषु च विनय: सर्वभूतानुकम्पा
    सामन्य: सर्वशास्त्रेष्वनुपहतविधि: श्रेयसामेष पन्था ॥

17. प्रदानं प्रच्छन्नं गृहमुपगते संभ्रमविधि:
    प्रियं कृत्वा मौनं सदसि कथनं चाप्यपकृते: ।
    अनुत्सेको लक्ष्म्यां निरभिभवसारा: परकथा:
    सतां केनादिष्टं विषममसिधारावृतमिदम् ॥

18. एते सत्पुरुषा: परार्थघटका: स्वार्थान्परित्यज्य ये
    यामान्यास्तु परार्थमुद्यमभृत: स्वार्थाविरोधेन ये ।
    नेऽमी मानवराक्षसा: परहितं स्वार्थाय निघ्नन्ति ये
    ये तु घ्नन्ति निरर्थकं परहितं ते केन जानीमहे ॥

19. क्षीरेणातमगतोदकाय हि गुणा: दत्ता: पुरा ते खिला:
    क्षीरोत्तापमवेक्ष्य तेन पयसा स्वात्मा कृशानौ हुत: ।
    गन्तुं पावकमुन्मनास्तदभवद् दृष्ट्वा तु मित्रापदं
    युक्तं तेन जलेन शाम्यति सतां मैत्री पुनस्त्वीदृशी ॥

20. तृष्णां छिन्धि भज क्षमां जहि मदं पापे रतिं मा कृथा:
    सत्यं ब्रूह्यनुयाहि साधुपदवीं सेवस्व विद्वज्जनम् ।
    मान्यान्मानय विद्विषोऽप्यनुनय प्रख्यापय स्वान्गुणान्
    कीर्तिं पालय दु:खिते कुरु दयामेतत्सतां लक्षणम् ॥

21. प्रारभ्यते न खलु विघ्नभयेन नीचै:-
    प्रारभ्य विघ्नविहता विरमन्ति मध्या: ।
    विघ्नै: पुन: पुनरपि प्रतिहन्यमाना:
    प्रारब्धमुत्तमजना न परित्यजन्ति ॥

22. आशा नाम नदी मनोरथजला तृष्णातरङ्गाकुला
    रागग्राहवती वितर्कविहगा धैर्यद्रुमध्वंसिनी ।
    मोहावर्तसुदुस्तराऽतिगहना प्रोत्तुङ्गचिन्तातटी
    तस्या: पारगता विशुद्धमनसो नन्दन्ति योगीश्वरा: ॥

23. भोगे रोगभयं कुले च्युतिभयं वित्ते नृपालाद्भयम्
    माने दैत्यभयं बले रिपुभयं रूपे जराया भयम् ।
    शास्त्रे वादभयं गुणे खलभयं काये कृतान्ताद्भयम्
    सर्वे वस्तु भयन्वितं भुवि नृणां वैराग्यमेवाभयम् ॥

Chapter XII

Ethics of Buddha

❀

In the history of every country great historical movements are preceded by the birth of one great historic personage, who, by his towering personality practically shapes the destinies of his nation. In India at a time when there was an intellectual ferment and when heretics, fanatics, agnostics and indifferentists were trying their level best to propound their own doctrines, and in fact, when the sun of Vedic philosophy was totally eclipsed by the shadow of ignorance, priestcraft and superstition, Buddha, the Great, was born and in due course preached a philosophy of life which at once created a mighty revolution in the social and political condition of Arya-Varta.

Notwithstanding the fact of historic criticism being unhappy as far as the details of his life are concerned there can be no doubt that Buddha is the brightest star in the galaxy of Indian reformers. Though born of an aristocratic class he led and preached the life of an ordinary man levelling down all distinctions of caste, colour or creed. A philosophic critic shall, undoubtedly, pay homage to his dignified bearing, his high intellectual endowments, his keen penetrating glance and his tremendous oratorical powers. A student of ethics will be lost in admiration at his gentleness,

frankness, liberality and his spotless life. He never professed
to be anything more than a man and always employed unique
methods of propagandism. He was sincerely desirous of rescuing
mankind from the fetters of greed, avarice and bigotry. He had
unbounded faith in the real endeavours of any man earnestly
seeking renunciation without leading a life of dreamy quietism
and grim asceticism. Ethical enlightenment, he rightly believed,
was sufficient to obtain NIRVANA. Love to all sentient beings was
the key to his philosophy and religion. He was an optimist of
optimists believing in the intrinsic greatness of man's capacity
to work out his salvation, independent of extraneous aid. The
rationality and the morality of Buddhism have brought solace
and comfort to millions of men in and outside India. If there be
a soul of truth in the saying that the marrow of civilised society
is ethical and not so much metaphysical, then surely Buddhism
even in the land of its birth, stands a fair chance of a revival.
Who can deny that, with the spread of education it will not give
rise to a new power for the unification of races? Who cannot
subscribe to the view of an eminent student of Buddhism that,
not till the 'White Light' of Buddha has once again penetrated
into the thought and life of an Indian, can they—Indians—hope
to regain that pre-eminence amongst nations that they possessed
in the time of Asoka? As an ethical system it may differ in certain
points from the system of Brahmanism and Vedantism but in broad
outlines his system of practical ethics is undoubtedly a CHILD
of Vedism. The fundamental doctrines of truthfulness, charity,
philanthropy, justice, tolerance and fraternity are but the echoes
of the preachings of the sublime Vedas and the Upanishads. What
wonder then that he has found a place in the Hindu pantheon?
A rapid survey of the morality of Buddhism will enable a Hindu
student to realise that Buddha is the blood of his blood and the
bone of his bone.

The end and aim of Buddhism is the freedom from sorrow and suffering which is only attainable by the destruction of all selfish cravings of an individual. Generally TRISHNA—greed—is the predominant feeling in a man and that deserves suppression. This annihilation of TRISHNA is possible only by the continual avoidance of all evil and the doing of good. The following are the ten precepts which Buddha taught for the guidance of his followers:–

I. From the meanest worm upto man you shall kill no animal but shall have regard for all life.

   This precept is mainly responsible for the propagation of the doctrine condemning the sacrifice of animal life which was a feature of the degenerate period of Vedism. Not only did Buddhism abhor the vain destruction of life but also it regarded care for the well-being of all animals as the most sacred duty. Accordingly we find in the second edict of Asoka that, in his dominions, mention has been made of hospitals for human beings as well as for animals. The spirit of toleration is another result of this precept. By peaceful means alone was Buddhism spread throughout the eastern and the southern part of Asia.

II. You shall neither steal nor rob, but help everyone to be the master of the fruits of his labour.

   In the DHAMMAPADA and the DHAMMIKA SUTTA we find similar principles enunciated in quite unequivocal terms. Whatever a genuine Buddhist earns by hard labour is to be spent for the benefit of mankind and hence it is that the Buddhist BHIKSHU—a monk—observes the vow of poverty. This noble precept can be easily perceived to be entirely opposed to the spirit of industrialism with its concomitant of merciless struggle for sordid pelf and power.

III. You shall not violate the wife of another, nor even his concubine, but lead a life of chastity.

'Guard against looking on a woman with an evil eye. If the woman be old regard her as your mother; if young, as your sister and if very young, as your child.'

In all religions we observe that the excesses connected with the satisfaction of sexual appetite have a feeling of sinfulness attached to them. Social efficiency requires that rules must be framed to regulate sexual relations. Marriages are not to be contracted solely with regard to the personal interests of the contracting parties but for the preservation of the species. KAMA, therefore, forms the third of the four objects of life according to Hindu Theology, but its improper exercise has given it a place among the SHADRIPUS—six enemies—KAMA, KRODHA, MOHA, LOBHA, MADA and MATSARA—Lust, Anger, Illusion, Greed, Pride and Jealousy.

IV. You shall speak no word that is false, but shall speak the truth, not so as to harm any but with a loving heart for all. 'When one comes to an assembly one should not tell lies to any one or cause any to tell any lies or consent to the acts of those who tell lies. One should avoid untruth.' DHAMMIKA SUTTA.

'Speak the truth: do not yield to anger: give if you are asked: by these three steps you will become divine.'—DHAMMAPADA

This precept condemns hypocrisy, calumny, perjury, and other forms of lying. Buddhism can by no means approve of the quackery of physicians, the chicanery of lawyers and the lying of diplomats.

V. You shall not eat or drink anything that may intoxicate:

That Drunkenness is the cause of many crimes has been acknowledged by religionists as well as scientists. Medical science is unanimous in its condemnation of intoxicating drugs and religion is equally strong on this point.

VI. You shall not swear or indulge in idle or vain talk but speak decently, speak with dignity and to the purpose, or keep silence.

VII. You shall not invent evil reports or repeat them. You shall not carp but look for the good side of your fellow-beings, so that you may with sincerity defend them against their enemies.

VIII. You shall not covet your neighbour's good but rejoice at the fortunes of other people.

Jealousy is to be avoided which is described as 'the fire of endless night, the fire that burns and gives no light'.

IX. You shall cast out all malice, anger, spite and ill-will, and shall not cherish hatred even against those who do you harm but embrace all living beings with loving kindness and benevolence. 'Let a man overcome anger by love: let him overcome evil by good. Let him overcome the greedy by liberality, and the liar by truth. For hatred does not cease by hatred at anytime: hatred ceases by love, this is its true nature' —DHAMMAPADA.

X. You shall free your mind of ignorance and be anxious to learn truth, lest you fall a prey to doubt which will make you indifferent to errors and which will lead you astray from the noble path that leads to blessedness and peace.

The following are the sins to be avoided: (a) Killing a living being—प्राणातिपाद (b) Stealing—अदत्तदान (c) Committing adultery—कास मिथ्याचार (d) Lying—मृषावाद (e) Slander—पैशुन्य (f) Abusive language (g) Frivolous talk—शंथिन्न प्रलाप (h) Avidya अविद्या—Ignorance, (i) Evil intent, (j) False view—मिथ्या दृष्टि .

Buddhism recognises reason to be the ultimate criterion of truth, Buddha says:—

'Do not believe in traditions merely because they have been handed down for many generations. . . . After observation and analysis, when it agrees with reason and is conducive to the good and benefit of one and

all, then accept it and live up to it.' The popular GATHA
summarises Buddhist ethics thus:–

सब्बपापस्स अकरणं कुसलस्स उपसंपदा ।
सचित्तपरियोदपनं एतं बुद्धानं सासनम् ॥

Let no evil be done, let good deeds be replenished. Let one's
heart be purified. These are the exhortations of Buddha.

The positive rules of ethical conduct are the following:–

(1) DANA—discriminate charity, (2) SILA BHAVANA—Purifying
moral conduct, (3) VEYYAVACCHA—Thinking of good things.
(4) APACHAYANA—Service of others, (5) PATTIPATTANU MODANA—
asking others to share with us in doing good, giving the merits
of one's good deeds to others, (6) DHAMMA SAVANA—Hearing the
Good Law, (7) DHAMMA DESANA—Preaching the Good Law.

Anagarika Dharmapala in his book, *The Life and Teachings
of Buddha*, admirably summarises the spirit of Buddhism.
'Buddhism is the Religion of earnest unswerving effort. It looks
to no god or gods, and asks for no extraneous help, except that
of one's own purity of conduct and unselfishness. "Look to no
extraneous aid, make yourself an island, depend on none, depend
on your own righteous exertions, and the supreme effort made
with earnestness to control the low nature is sure to succeed.
Strive earnestly, persevere strenuously, let no lethargy, irritability
and scepticism prevent you from reaching the goal. Ring out
the old, ring in the new, avoid evil, store in the good. Fight
valiantly against sin, lust and selfishness."' Buddhism teaches that
man can attain Nirvana in this life but that he must stand on the
foundations of IDHIPADA and develop faith, attentiveness, energy
and concentration of good thoughts and wisdom. Dr Ananda
Coomaraswamy, too, in his recent book on Buddhism, arrives at
a similar conclusion. The following is the well-known Eight-fold
Noble Path, which is the absolute way to reach the goal, and
its principles are: (1) Right Knowledge, (2) Right Aspirations,

(3) Right Speech, (4) Right Actions, (5) Right Livelihood, (6) Right Endeavour, (7) Right Attention, and (8) Right Samadhi.

We quote below a few verses from DHAMMAPADA, a canonical book of the Buddhists, as translated by Prof Max-Müller in his *Sacred Books of the East*.

1. All that we are is the result of what we have thought:–
    It is founded on our thoughts, it is made up of our thoughts.
    If a man speaks or acts with an evil thought, pain follows him, as the wheel following the foot of the ox that draws the carriage.

    (Verse 1.)

2. Earnestness is the path of immortality, thoughtlessness the path of death. Those who are in earnest do not die, those who are thoughtless are as if they are dead already.

    (Verse 22.)

3. Those wise people, meditative, steady, always possessed of strong powers, attain to Nirvana, the highest happiness.

    (Verse 23)

4. Let the wise man guard his thoughts, for they are difficult to perceive, very artful and they rush wherever they list; thoughts well-guarded bring happiness.

    (Verse 36.)

5. Fools of poor understanding have themselves for their greatest enemies, for they do evil deeds which bear bitter fruits

    (Verse 66.)

6. As a solid rock is not shaken by the wind, wise people falter not amidst blame and praise.

    (Verse 81.)

7. The gods even envy him whose senses, like horses well broken in by the driver, have been subdued, who is free from pride and free from appetites.

    (Verse 94.)

8. Let no man think lightly of good, saying in his heart it will not come unto me. Even by the falling of water-drops a water-pot is filled; the wise man becomes full of good, even if he gather it little by little.

(Verse 122-)

9. Not nakedness, not plaited hair, not dirt, not fasting or lying on earth, not rubbing with dust, not sitting motionless, can purify a mortal who has not overcome desires.

(Verse 141.)

10. Health is the greatest of gifts, contentment the best riches, trust is the best of relationship, Nirvana the highest happiness.

(Verse 204.)

11. Let a man overcome anger by love, evil by good, the greedy by liberality, and the liar by truth.

(Verse 223.)

In Dhammapada there are 423 verses preaching virile and purifying ethics. The very word DHAMMAPADA means 'The Paths of Religion', and the book as a whole is an excellent treatise on Buddhistic Ethics. The SUTTA-NIPATA is another canonical book of the Buddhists which is a collection of discourses on subjects of ethical importance from the standpoint of primitive Buddhism. It contains good many parables which enunciate and illustrate the principles of Buddhism. What is sin? In what does bliss consist? These and similar other questions have been raised and answered. It vividly describes the life of a hermit in the first stage and is by itself an important contribution to the right understanding of primitive Buddhism. V. Fansböll has given the following analysis, of the contents of SUTTA-NIPATA:

'Bliss, subjectively is emancipation from desire by means of the peace which Buddha preaches objectively, it is emancipation from body and matter. One must destroy the elements of existence, UPADHI and obtain NIRVANA.' Buddha preached the Gospel of all-embracing Love and Wisdom. He was at first struck by pain, misery, despair, decay, disease, dissolution and disintegration in this world and then by a process of unique self-culture discovered the cause and the cessation thereof. A people determined to reach the highest realms of truth and righteousness can profitably study the life and the teachings of this great master of morals. Buddha was a supreme type of the great sage, and one of those supreme manifestations of the great Life Force on this planet of ours who, from time to time, adorn our race. His teachings are essentially and emphatically moral. Their aim is to inculcate, and to make supreme, the highest moral motives. The gospel of moral reformation which Buddhism preaches and which gives to man self-mastery and marked development of individuality is a successful attempt at a universal religion. Every student of sociology knows full well that the world has always been marching towards progress and unification, and in this process of evolution it strives after a unified creed also. The contribution which Buddhism has made to this world-wide creed is undeniably great.

The work of Buddha has been continued down the centuries by a succession of great spiritual teachers in and outside India. In India, from time to time, mighty intellects have been born and carried the torch of spiritual enlightenment throughout the length and breadth of the country. Saints like Chaitanya, Kabir, Ramadas and Tukaram, have prescribed to human life fixed principles of action and fixed rules of conduct. In days of languor and gloom, as well as in the days of our sunshine and energy, their devotional songs pitched in immortal strains, are a source of inspiration. To many a sailor on this ocean of life they are the very beacon lights. They are in more senses than one, spokesmen and prophets of the human family. They have administered to the comforts of their fellow-beings and mitigated human miseries. 'We may be sure that, in proportion as we master their works and imbibe their spirit, we shall ourselves become in our own measure the ministers of like benefits to others, be they many or few, be they in the obscurer or the more distinguished walks of life.'

Chapter XIII

The Ethical Religion
of the Hindus

❧

Hinduism is more a civilisation than a religion. It has a distinct cultural mission of its own, unique alike in conception and development. The holy scriptures, extracts from which have been given in the previous chapters, provide the data on which a system of ancient ethics can be built up. In them are recorded the experience of their authors in the form of moral precepts for the guidance of people in general. If throughout the long and chequered history of Hinduism the people at times have failed to act up to those grand ideals and through selfishness or ignorance they have given the go-by to all the fundamental principles of their religion none need point the finger of scorn either at the authors or the religion. The history of every religion has all along been presenting one curious chapter. It seems as though the phenomenon is inevitable. The founders of religions place before their followers certain definite ideals of life and preach certain rules of conduct. Having dedicated their lives to a certain cause, either of God or their country they pass away having partially or wholly accomplished their life work but their followers prompted by lust or greed abandon the path of righteousness chalked out for them by these masterminds and naturally an age of hypocrisy and insincerity sets in. Essentials of religion are soon forgotten and the non-essentials ring in the era of superstitious beliefs and meaningless dogmas. The lower nature of man asserts itself and the *Surasura Sangram* (सुरासुरसंग्राम) commences in all its hideousness. Our SANATANA DHARMA, too, has shared this miserable fate so common to all the religions and long ago entered upon a career of keen struggles with the alien systems of thought. The main question is how far religion by itself is responsible for the existence of the enormous volume of wickedness and misery. When all the founders of religions, prophets, saints and philosophers struggled and scrambled to mitigate misery and pain in the world why is it that evil still persists? A particular form of religion might have brought solace and comfort to certain individuals but are nations and races saved by religious beliefs? Has religion any chance of ridding the world of its miseries and tribulations? What is the panacea for all the ills of life? Hinduism answers 'Preserve DHARMA and you preserve everything'; 'Seek the kingdom of God and Righteousness'; 'Strive to attain SVARGA-RAJYA' and the riddle of the Universe is solved. Attain BRAHMA-ANANDA eternal bliss. Drink deep at the ETERNAL FOUNTAIN of ETERNAL BLISS and then will the Great purpose of life be realised. What is this SANATANA DHARMA? Let us humbly and reverently seek the answer from the history of Hindu thought, Hindu ethics and Hindu religion, carefully bearing in mind the fact that so far as Hinduism is concerned all these are identical. There is no divorce between Hindu religion and Hindu ethics. So we prefer to give this chapter the heading of the 'ETHICAL RELIGION OF THE HINDUS'.

The cultural mission of Hinduism, the sublimity of its teachings, its grand ideals and soul-elevating sentiments, its beneficent rules of conduct, its social organisation, its VARNA-ASHRAMA Dharma, its SADHANA-CHATUSHTAYAS, its PANCHA-MAHAYAJNAS, its SODASHA-SAMSKARAS, the message of its Vedas, the Upanishads, the Shastras and the PURANAS and lastly its noblest ideal of VEDANT, one and all, point to the great and substantial contribution to the history of human civilisation and also to the 'greatest good of the greatest number', which Hinduism has made and is making even now. The process is still going on and if irreconcilable rationalists are not prepared to accept the dictum that 'VEDANTA' is the last word on religion, sympathetic critics will have to admit that the Aryan race deserves a place in the comity of the nations of the world and its ethicists have lived to some purpose.

The ethical religion as propounded by the mighty seers of yore, the RISHIES of Ind, presupposes the acceptance of certain postulates and axioms relating to the NITI-DHARMA (ethical religion). If these be not accepted and if this NITI-DHARMA be subjected to the crossfire of criticism by standards other than these, both the student and the critic of the Hindu ethics will force themselves into a hopelessly ridiculous position. If one cannot accept the postulates enunciated by Euclid or discard his axioms *in toto* one can never make any progress in the study of the sciences of geometry. If this be true of positive sciences like mathematics or physics, the acceptance of certain ethical postulates also becomes all the more essential before one ventures to study the spirit of Hindu ethics. If one discards the theory of Karma and the belief in the Transmigration of the Human Soul the attempt, however sympathetic and sincere it may be to sit in judgement over the moral Code of the Hindu thinkers, is bound to be futile. Exactly similar is the position of critics like Principal McKenzie. It is one thing to disbelieve such doctrines and it is quite a different thing to discredit a system of Hindu ethics which is after all based on these and similar doctrines. Let us try to refer to these postulates and axioms briefly and then summarise the ideals of the ethical religion.

1. God is the Creator of the Universe and also the Moral Governor. His universe is ruled by certain definite laws to which all the human beings should conform.

2. Every human soul has to go the rounds of births and deaths.

3. Every human soul is free to perform actions and reap the fruit thereof. Good KARMA will have and has its own reward and evil its own punishment.

4. NISHKAMA KARMA, action performed without the desire of reward, is the best and the highest form of action.

5. Attainment of Divine Bliss and the freedom of the soul from the bondage of matter are the objects of life.

6. MUKTI should be sought after by leading a life of benevolence and Virtue and conforming it to laws divine.

7. Service to fellow-beings (परोपकार) is the highest form of Virtue and the ideal of the five daily YAJNAS is one of disinterested service to fellowmen; the institution of SAMNYAS (संन्यास) is also conducive to the welfare of the Society as well as to that of the individual.

8. Life of action is the noblest of lives. Compare the ideal कुर्वन्नेवेह कर्माणि जिजीविषेत् शतँ समा:– 'Live for hundred years doing disinterested service.' परोपकाराय सतां विभूतय:. It is this sort of life which is desired to be led by the teachings of the BHAGAVAD GITA. There it is called KARMA-YOGA ultimately leading to Brotherhood of Man (लोकसंग्रह) .

9. There are three paths of attaining DIVINE BLISS, (i) KARMA-MARGA—Path of action (ii) JNANA-MARGA—Path of knowledge (iii) BHAKTI-MARGA—Path of disinterested devotion. All these three paths should combine for the pursuit of the Highest.

10. Non-Violence is the essence of Dharma. Freedom from injury in word, deed and thought is the noblest rule.

11. वेदाहमेतं पुरुषं महान्तम्
    आदित्यवर्णं तमस: परस्तात् ।
    तमेव विदित्वाऽतिमृत्युमेति
    नान्य: पन्था विद्यतेऽयनाय ॥श्वे.3.8.

'By knowing Him alone one can attain immortality. There is no other way of crossing the ocean of death. He is called the Great Person who shines beyond the region of darkness, with great splendour.'

12. 'Truth alone conquers', (सत्यमेव जयते).

13. Every devotee should pray for 'Peace,' 'Peace and Peace' everywhere. Prayers end invariably with this Mantra—SHANTI, SHANTI, SHANTI. It is not meant that the life should be one of passivity but one of universal love, peace and harmony.

Having enunciated these Hindu ethical postulates, let us proceed a step further. Why should we lead a moral life? What is the basis of Morality? Should we lead a moral life simply because it would make our neighbours' lives happier? Is happiness the basis of morality? Can we take, for instance, our individual happiness as the criterion of morality? If it were so, depriving other people of their property by means foul or fair may perhaps make us happy but is such happiness to be sought after? Hinduism denies it and the SHASTRAS condemn it. According to the Hindu SHASTRAS the basis of morality is to be sought after elsewhere. God is Omnipotent and All-just. The law of morality is an eternal and an unchangeable law of Nature. We mortals as worshipers of God cannot infringe the obligation of morality. Either reward or punishment should not be the basis of morality. If a man commits no theft simply because he is afraid of the police he cannot be said to be moral. He should not do it because it is unlawful and against God's Laws. On the other hand we should lead a life of goodness and righteousness notwithstanding the fact that such a life may demand of us the suffering of pain and miseries patiently. Such was the ideal with which the Great Harischandra modelled his life to keep up his promise. He suffered many privations and was submitted to all sorts of humiliations but in the end his ideal of Truth triumphed. Harischandra's greatness consists in the fact that he considered a life of Virtue essential, not because it did him good or brought him happiness but because it was the law of his being. Life of Sri Rama or Bharata was great and highly moral from this standpoint. All world's great men who have a claim on our reverence attained the position of eminence as moralists not because they cared for their individual happiness but because they cared more for virtue and righteousness in spite of the pains and losses which that life brought in its train. SHRIYALA's ideal of hospitality, Dilipa's ideal of devotion to his guru, Hanuman's ideal of service all come under the same category. The purpose of TAPAS-Penance——for achieving any object in life is also similar. Sita, Ahilya, Tara and Mandodari are the best jewels of Hindu womanhood because they were loyal for loyalty's sake. Indian history is brimful of the instances of men and women who sacrificed their all for the sake of righteousness at the altar of their country and religion, irrespective of consequences. If the system of ethics has produced such a galaxy of great men and women, it cannot be stigmatised as 'puerile, cold and lifeless'.

Morality of action also depends on the nature of the motives which prompted it. Many a time it becomes supremely difficult to discover a man's motive for doing a particular action. An action to be good, three conditions are essential (1) The action should be good by itself; (2) It should be prompted by good motive; and (3) It should be voluntary. Any action that is dictated by fear or coercion cannot be highly moral. Virtue practised for fear of any evil result degenerates into hypocricy. Love, charity, compassion and pity lose their greatness when they are tainted by selfishness, and no longer become virtues when the individual practising them has no moral intention. The end can never justify the means. If a subject is loyal for fear of the Penal Code, his loyalty cannot be said to be moral. If a capitalist raises the wages of his labourers for fear of a strike, his charitable disposition cannot be raised to the rank of a virtue. If luxuries are condemned for want of means to enjoy them, plain-living of such an ABHAVA-VAIRAGI is not a highly moral action. The classification of virtues as SATTVIKA, RAJASIKA and TAMASIKA is noteworthy and they are dealt with great length in the BHAGAVAD-GITA. A virtue to be noble and an action to be genuinely great they should be of the SATTVIKA (सात्त्विक) type only.

The science of Ethics does not deal with man as he is, but teaches him how he ought to be. The advancement of positive sciences has revealed to man the beauties of the external world but the science of ethics and religion, dealing as it does with conscience and man's relations with the society as a whole is yet in a stage of infancy. Man being swayed by influences of convention and at times his vision being blurred by selfishness fails to see that this universe is guided by laws, moral and divine. That law is above all man-made laws. God's law is supreme. It is eternal and immutable. The seat is within ourselves. Its centre is everywhere and circumference no where. It is absolutely independent of our likes and dislikes, it is far above and beyond our so-called conventions. Even nations are influenced by its inexorable effects. When nations forsake the path of righteousness terrible destructions await them. Their wealth, their power, their might and their pride are all humbled to dust. The Mahabharata War was preceded by an age of hypocricy, tyranny and unrighteousness. Similar was the history and the final fate of Ravana's empire. The empires of Assyria, Babylon, Greece, Rome, France of pre-Revolution days and Germany of pre-war days establish once again the fact that Society is more based on moral foundations than on armaments or military strength. No man, much less a nation can violate the Great Moral Law with impunity. If he or they tread the path of virtue and righteousness. peace, freedom, contentment and happiness will fall to their lot. Such is the ideal of the Hindu ethical religion. Even Darwin, the propounder of the doctrine of the 'Survival of the Fittest' recognises that there is a vital connection between morality and the external world. Even the lower animals show unmistakable signs of the existence in them of the moral instinct. Intellectual strength is undeniably greater than physical strength but moral strength is incontrovertibly superior to even intellectual strength. So Darwin's theory, instead of being antagonistic to the Hindu ideal of 'DHARMA-RAKSHA' is supporting it and exalts righteousness and veracity far above wealth, pelf or power.

The Hindu ideal of morality demands that service to humanity is the noblest function of man. 'आत्मवत् सर्वभूतेषु यः पश्यति स पश्यति'—'He who considers all human beings as his own self is the real seer.' In the Gayatri-Mantra the repetition of which is enjoined on every Hindu it is said धियो यो नः प्रचोदयात्—'Guide our intellect in the path of righteousness.' The Vedas declare संगच्छध्वं संवध्वं संवो मनांसि जानतां—'Let us go together, let us speak together, let us all be of one mind. 'The plural नः is very significant. It is not individual progress that is sought after but the welfare of the whole society that is earnestly desired and fervently prayed for. The ethics of the VEDANTA with its principle of 'Thou art that' is the highest and the noblest conception of the Hindu ethical religion. We are part and parcel of that Supreme Soul which is also Truth and Purity. Practise these virtues as ordained by 'Divine Moral Law', A certain school of thought holds that ethics is the means whereby a religious life can be fully developed. Whether we regard ethics as a means of religion or as part and parcel of religion one thing is certain that a life of righteousness alone is the life that deserves to be led. 'What shall it profit a man if he gains the whole world and loses his own soul'?—मृतं शरीरं उत्सृज्य काष्ठलोष्ठसमंवत्-विमुखा बान्धवा यान्ति धर्मस्त्वमनुगच्छति Only 'Dharma' will follow you and everything else will be left behind. We have in our Introduction referred to other aspects of Hindu ethics and need not. Therefore, repeat them here. When we say that the ethical religion from the Hindu standpoint is the best religion that can bring solace and comfort to man we do not deny that there may be other systems equally potent and great. That very same religion which preaches tolerance and as a proof of which we see today that under the spreading branch of Hinduism several other 'isms' like monotheism and polytheism are included demands of us not to indulge in diatribes against other systems. All that we hold is that, at least for the Hindus with the social environments and religious tendencies peculiar to the race, this system of the ethical religion is bound to result in their goodness and greatness. We are not blind to the fact that the moral law knows no geographical boundaries and racial distinctions. It is of universal application but all the same the requirements of the Hindu race and its aspirations are bound to be satisfied, if in practice this ethical religion were to influence them in the way in which it did men and women of yore. The crown, the 'Hinduism' need not be any other 'ity or ism'. The crown is there. Only it should be worn. The practical life should be modelled on the lines of righteousness and then none need despair of this race which has through thick and thin preserved its distinct cultural mission for ages together. The vitality of the Hindu civilisation by itself is a proof positive of the greatness of its ETHICAL DHARMA.*

---

* We are indebted to a part of this chapter to Mr Gandhi's booklet on the subject.

Chapter XIV

A Note on Principal McKenzie's Book on 'Hindu ethics'

ॐ

Over the whole civilised world a flood-tide of dissatisfaction seems to come surging which the advance of natural sciences has tried in vain to resist. The deepest problems of life and death have remained unsolved. The riddle of man's destiny has become more and more perplexing. Materialism, the parent of all revolutions and wars, has entered upon a most subtle and deadly warfare. The whole fabric of civilisation seems tottering. But 'the cloud has a silver lining'. The counter-current of spirituality seems also to have set in. Is it not probable that from the East a mighty tributary may flow into this counter-current and stem the tide of materialism? If the Eastern thought should be properly interpreted to the West it is quite probable that with the united labours of the Eastern and the Western SAVANTS the source of the New Light meant to illumine the murky road of life may soon be traced. From this standpoint the historical and the critical essay by Prof McKenzie on 'Hindu Ethics' deserves a careful study. But religious thought in Hindu India has developed on so amazingly perplexing lines that no amount of 'sincere and scientific spirit' is adequate to realise the significance of the age-long quest of the

Indian for religious truth. Hinduism with its ascetic, devotional and mystic elements, its remarkable social organisation and its vast and varied literature defies any attempt to present a trustworthy account of its intricate problems. The task is certainly as stupendous as it is hazardous. Prof MaKenzie has attempted it and while we admire his labours and appreciate his sincerity of purpose we feel that he has not done full justice to the subject. For one thing he assumes superiority of Christian ethics and 'damns Hindu ethics with faint praise.' Such an attitude seems incompatible with the aims with which the writer and the general editor want to deal with a subject so wide and complicated as 'Hindu Ethics'. If to men of his thinking 'Jesus Christ has become the light of all their seeing and they believe Him destined to be the light of all their seeing and they believe Him destined to be light of the world'—we have no quarrel with them. It is a matter of their faith and it is no business of ours to question it. If in a separate volume the greatness of Christian ethics by itself was established we should have nothing but praise for the author's labour of love but when attempts are made to institute comparisons and to establish the superiority of one system of thought over another we feel we should make our own humble and respectful protest against such 'odious comparisons.' If in our attempt to establish the greatness of 'Hindu ethics' we were to run down all other systems of thought, like Hebrew, Islamic or Christian, we would have cut a very sorry and ridiculous figure. A spirit of bias can hardly be called scientific. We are sorry that the last five or six chapters of the book bear unmistakable signs of such an 'injudicious attitude.' When men of the type of Rev McKenzie's scholarship approach the study of Hindu ethics with the avowed object of finding out how that system falls short of Christianity, we feel that the days of sympathetic criticism are gone and the dreams of thinkers like Raja Ram Mohan Roy and Dr. Rabindranath Tagore, as well as the visions of saints, like

Nanak and Kabir are more or less empty and unreal. Sturdy optimists who are expecting the wonderful confluence of the three great streams of Hinduism, Islam and Christianity are bound to receive a rude shock.

For the sake of argument let us assume that Christian ethic is entirely free from defects and ideal in every way and that Christainity is the 'Crown of Hinduism' and at the same time presume that modern civilisation is the natural outcome of Christianity. Where shall such an assumption lead us to? Let us wipe the dust of prejudice from our eyes and look facts squarely in the face. Western nations have become the rulers of vast empires. Positive sciences have made a remarkable advance and man has won triumphs over nature. Inert matter and invisible forces of nature have SURRENDERED their secrets to man. How and where was 'the golden key' to open these hidden treasures found? How could the Westerners claim the sovereignty of two-third of the habitable world? To what extent is the 'sermon on the Mount' responsible for the militarism and the industrialism of the West? For fear of being styled as dogmatic we do not endeavour to answer these querries. The terrible European War of 1914 and its after-effects have given a simple and a straight answer—'Materialism has been tried in a manner it was never tried before and has been found wanting.' Why should a system of ethics so sound and so perfect produce such a melancholy result? Of course victory was a triumph of the cause of righteousness but why were the forces of evil so terrific? Should we pass the dictum that the ethics was entirely defective?

Then again while discussing the merits of Christian ethics and the defects of Hindu ethics, the leanered author seems to have viewed the whole question from the standpoint of western ethicists. The Hindu standpoint is fundamentally different from this. To a Hindu with his favourite doctrines of MAYA and MUKTI, the BRAHMAN is beyond good and evil. In the West they seem to make God and the good identical. To a Hindu the realm of morality seems restricted to the domain of this topsy-turvy world and ethics is only a step towards the realisation of the BRAHMAN which is गुणातीत, 'GUNA-TITA'. 'NITI is only a SADHANA and God is the SADHYA'. Without clearly bearing in mind this fundamental difference we regret Prof McKenzie has passed an injudicious dictum on 'Hindu Ethics'.

Thirdly, the author believes and perhaps rightly too that this Hindu attitude to 'beyond good and evil' is dangerous. We do not deny that it may afford an excuse for a moral wrong-doer but let us not leave human nature out of account. A doctrine may be ethically pure but in practice people may override it and perpetrate atrocities. It may be either due to their intellectual laziness or to perverted mentality. The cult of SHAKTI-PUJA may have abuses, the custom of sacrifices may be cruel, the Vama-margis may have monstrous customs, Lord Buddha's doctrine of AHIMSA (अहिंसा) may have degenerated into an abominable form of hypocricy, Lord Krishna's 'Gopi-lila' may be responsible for many evil practices but the main question is how far ethics by itself is responsible for all these curious and ugly phases. If we base our conclusions on these arguments and make sweeping statements, we shall be doing a distinct disservice to the cause of fair criticism and even to ethics itself. Would it not be an insult, nay even sacrilege, to Christ if his ethics were condemned for the monstrocities of the inquisition for the black deeds of the popes against which Luther or Zwingli led a relentless war, for the sinking of the Lusitania or the bombing of the civil population during the last Titanic stiuggle? We do not say this in defence of the evil practices existing in the Hindu society or for the matter of that in any society but only state the facts as they are. The ethics places before us the ideals of how we ought to be and if in practice people fall short of these ideals and are what they are, who can be held responsible for this curious state of affairs? A Manu, a Krishna or a Christ, does not deserve to be condemned for their so-called admirers' delinquency any more than the framers of the Penal Code for the atrocities of a gang of thugs or dacoits.

Fourthly, the professor holds that Hinduism has not solved the mystery of life. To us at any rate it seems as though the problems of life and death and the mystery of human destiny are eternal problems. No final word has been said or can be said on these perpetually perplexing riddles. All the world religions have endeavoured to give certain solutions but they are only partial. At the most the great good that they have done is to bring to their followers a certain amount of solace and comfort and cheer them up in this perilous voyage of life. To say that one religion in preference to another has given the final solution of these everlasting and age-long problems is to show an utter forgetfulness of the finiteness of human nature. That a finite mind with all the limitations and the disabilities born of this finiteness should be able to fully realise the Infinite is an impossibility. Not that the quest and the search are in vain but that the spiritual thirst can only be partially satiated is what we hold. If Hinduism has not solved the mystery of life we respectfully ask the author which religion has done or can do it? Has Christianity done it or has it given rise to further mysteries? To solve one mystery another mystery has been invented. It has become more a question of multiplication of mysteries than the solution of one particular mystery. The Upanishads say,' त्वमेव विदित्वा अतिमृत्युमेति, पन्था विद्यते अयनाय—By knowing Him alone everything else will be known." The VEDANTA says 'THOU ART THAT'. The mystics and saints of India have given their own answers which we have referred to in another chapter on 'THEISM OF INDIAN SAINTS' (Chapter XV). The learned author refers to the personal relationship conceived as existing between whether social or individualistic do not by themselves seem to be productive of ideal good. The history of European civilisation is presenting as sad a commentary on the efficacy of Christian ethics as the history of Hindu civilisation on the efficacy of Hindu ethical systems. Individualistic tendencies and social tendencies have taken tortuous courses, in spite of these gospels. The causes seem to lie far deeper. History in all ages and climes has taken its own course setting aside all these gospels and brushing aside all the cobwebs woven by human bigotry, ingenuity and selfishness. In spite of all these religions, is it not remarkable that history should take its own course? Is it not a unique and an inexplicable phenomenon? A detailed review of the book, chapter by chapter, seems both unnecessary and tedious. To realise the beauty of a flower, like the rose, it is imperative that it should be viewed as a whole. If from a rose petal after petal were to be plucked, it is possible that its beauty will be marred and the thorns may look more prominent. That flower which is known as 'the Queen of flowers' will then present an ugly appearance. Not dissimilar is the position taken up by Prof McKenzie when he endeavours to trace the materials essential for the building up of a history of Hindu ethics, through the Vedas, the Upanishads and the Six Schools of Philosophy. If oriental scholars look down upon the Vedas as the 'babblings of a human race sunk in primeval ignorance'——there are Indian scholars and commentators like. Arabindo Ghose, Pandit Gurudatta Vidyarthi who believe that the terminology of the Vedas needs a thorough revision. The meanings of Vedic terms are to be ascertained from two entirely different standpoints—YOGIC and RUDHIC—and then alone will the oriental scholars realise why the VEDAS are considered as 'Revealed Scriptures' and why they are said to contain 'DECIDEDLY NINETEENTH CENTURY-LIKE IDEAS'. The subject of the Vedic terminology is a vast and a complicated one and it is futile to attempt and refute the allegations made or conclusions drawn by the author based on a terminology of doubtful correctness. So we have thought it fit to review the book in general terms only.

From these general observations on the trend of thought in the book let us proceed to examine two other doctrines of Hinduism, which have naturally formed the target of Prof McKenzie's criticism. These two fundamental doctrines, one of KARMA and the other of TRANSMIGRATION or Reincarnation of human soul are allied, Karma being 'the companion truth of Reincarnation'. The learned author has devoted one full chapter to the 'Scientific examination' of these two doctrines. Before we proceed to examine the fallacies of the arguments so ingeniously put forward by the author we should like to add a word or two as an exposition of these basic principles of Hindu thought. Without a clear understanding of what they really mean and signify, it is futile to condemn a system of ethics built upon these theories. One may not feel inclined to place implicit faith in them but it is dangerous to find flaws in a system which is their natural outcome.

Reincarnation is a simple doctrine rooted in the belief of the soul's indestructibility. It teaches us that the soul enters this life, not as a fresh creation but after a long course of previous existences on this planet and perhaps on other heavenly bodies, in which it has acquired its present peculiarities and is also on its way to future transformations. The human soul is not a mere cohesion of atomic forces resulting in this personality soon to dissolve again into the elements but it is an eternal entity impressed with undecipherable ancentral inscriptions revealed in their moulding influence upon new careers. 'We are heirs of all the ages' and our past, present and future have flown by the great law of cause and effect from the accumulated momentum of past KARMA—impulses, aspirations and actions. In this wonderful universe there is no special favouritism but all will have equal facilities for future growth and steady progress. Suffering now patiently borne will produce a vast treasure of patience and fortitude in another life. Hardships will give rise to strength, self-denial will lead to the development of will and tastes, cultivated and acquired now will bear fruit in the coming lives. Similarly, our present uncontrollable impulses, peculiar tendencies, favourite pursuits and the soul-stirring friendships have all descended from our age-long previous activities. From the dawn of history the doctrine has dominated the minds of all the primitive races and it has held its unquestioned sway over all the mighty thinkers of all ages and climes. The ancient civilisations of Egypt, Greece and India, the philosophies of Pythagoros, Plato, Virgil and Ovid—the neo-platonism of Plotinus, the religion of the Persian Magi, the transcendental philosophy of the Upanishads, the metampsychosis of the Druids and the Gauls, the civilisations of Peru and Mexico, the priestly ceremonials of the Egyptian Isis, the Eleusinian mysteries of Greece, the Bacohic processions of Rome, the Cabalic rituals of the Hebrews, all bear eloquent testimony to the wonderful potentiality of this doctrine.* Two-thirds of the human race have tenaciously clung to this notion. Is not such a hoary philosophy cherished by theological leaders, like Julius Muller, scientists, like Flammarion and philosophers, like Kant and Schopenhaur, worthy of our profoundest respect or at least of sympathetic study?

Likewise, the doctrines of KARMA this Law of Causation is exceedingly simple. In a lucid way it pleads that we are what we are by our former actions and the builders of our future by our present. There is no destiny but what we ourselves determine. There is no salvation except what we ourselves bring about. God has placed at our disposal all the powers and the handle by which we use them to build our future is our own individual will. The KARMA of our ATMAN is performed even in the inner consciousness and the vocal expression or the outward act is the propelling force which directs our journey through infinity, whether it be into the dark regions of evil or into the sunny

---

* Walker's Re-incarnation.

fields of good and love. Then comes into operation the great Law of Moral Equity and the 'Sense of Moral responsibility in Man' of Kant. The Universal sustainer—THE VISHNU of the Hindu Trinity—gives every creature his due and the self-same Moral Governor has ordained 'Work out your own Salvation'. Whatsoever a man soweth, that shall he also reap. If St. Paul preaches this doctrine and if Jesus Christ sanctions it, why should it be of less worth when Krishna upholds it?

We admit this is a stern law and perhaps it may not arouse feelings of satisfaction in the hearts of those who believe in such doctrines as 'Vicarious atonement, intercession, forgiveness and death-bed conversions'. But man should be made of sterner stuff and then alone he can move on smoothly on the path of progress. Weaker tenets may lead to stagnation and decay. Ethical life stands for progressive evolution towards a spiritual life and the doctrine of Karma cannot be said to retard that progress. With these few preliminary remarks let us proceed to examine one or two special objections raised by the author. This doctrine is said to be 'inconsistent with the idea of Grace of God' which is prominently traceable in the BHAKTI Literature. But the lives of saints and mystics, like Kabir, Tukaram and Ramakrishna Paramahamsa, illustrate that it is possible to overcome even KARMA by BHAKTI. Justice and mercy are not antagonistic. Even a just man can be merciful and the doctrine of KARMA never says that God's Mercy need not be sought for and recognised. Does it not also suggest that sins need not be committed and His Mercy sought for in vain? There is no room, holds the author, in this doctrine for 'Vicarious suffering'? Perhaps not. But the ideas of TAPAS—Penance—and YAMA and NIYAMA are so prominent in the literature of the Hindus that none need feel sorry for the absence of this aspect of ethical life. How far sins committed may be forgiven if any other individual suffers misery for their sake is yet to be established. Rationalism rejects the doctrine.

The author says that it is immoral to punish a man for actions of which he has no recollection. Believers in the doctrines of Karma and rebirth consider that this forgetfulness is a blessing and is natural. If we should all remember every detail of the happenings of past births our lives would be miserable indeed. And after all, how far can our memory retain the impression. They are bound to fade away. We are glad to note the author making this happy remark—'This doctrine emphasises action and not character.' We are in entire agreement with the first part of the quotation and as for the second part we confess our inability to grasp the exact meaning of the words 'not character'. But why? Is not action the outcome of character and is not character in turn, moulded or influenced by action ?

Our remarks should not lead one to conclude that Prof McKenzie has never emphasised the good points of the Science of Hindu Ethics. He shows sympathy and admiration for BHAKTAS, like Kabir and Ramanuia, and he has a kind word for some of the modern movements and their line of work. But as the reader goes through the concluding chapters he feels that there is a lack of imaginative sympathy as also of sympathetic vision in handling such a subject as 'Hindu Ethics'. But the treatment is quite in accordance with the second aim of the author, though to us, it seems, that the first aim and the second aim are quite incompatible. The book, however, is bound to rouse the interest of the Western people in the study of the ethical literature of the world. The angle of vision alone needs a change and we trust by the time the second edition of the book is issued that angle will have considerably changed and the presentation of the subject will be more scientific and sympathetic, the inferences more considerate, the conclusions more accurate and the judgements less severe. Before we conclude this lengthy note let us assure both the patient reader and the learned author that we have penned these lines with the best of intentions and never with any malicious desire to prolong these controversies. The author has as much right to place his side of the case as we have to place our own. The reader, however, is in the more enviable position of drawing his own conclusions. The law of parallelogram of forces acts with as much force in mechanics as it does in the world of thought. When two forces act and re-act on a certain theme truth becomes the resultant. Is it too much to hope that this note will serve the purpose of ascertaining the truth?

Chapter XV

Theism of Indian Saints

The muster-roll of the benefactors of humanity has in it many names of saints carved in letters of gold. These were men of disinterested piety who dedicated their lives to the cause of God and their fellowmen. There are evidences to show that such men lived and died even in 'prehistoric India'. They were neither those intellectual giants bent upon founding new sects nor were they those keen-witted theologians determined to open new schools of philosophy. They did not even belong to the type of those much maligned SADHUS who under the cloak of religion preferred to lead the life of social parasites. First and foremost, they were servants of society and therefore devotees of God. Their devotional fervour burning at white heat was equalled only by their sincere desire to ameliorate the condition of fallen brethren. With a firm faith in Divine goodness and greatness they most humbly and reverently sought for His mercy. With a tremendous soul-force generated in the furnace of VAIRAGYA they served humanity breaking all the social conventions and communal restrictions, if these chanced to stand between man and God. Ecstacy born of a passionate devotion to a Personal God was their only solace in life. Joy felt in the company of their fellow-believers was their only comfort in the world. They were known as BHAKTAS and their religion as 'BHAGAVATA-DHARMA'. Their theism, to use the words of Matthew Arnold, was some thing of 'Morality touched with emotion'. To borrow Plato's phrase they belived 'God is the only reality'. While some declared 'All is God', others held that 'God is all'. Some went a step further and held that 'God is beyond good and evil'. It is practically impossible to characterise their theism by any particular appellation as pantheism or dualism. It is a curious combination of all these. Its roots go far down into mysticism and branches shoot off above idealism. In it the mythical element is not entirely absent and the ethical element presents itself only as a step towards the realisation of the *Summum Bonum* of life, viz., the attainment of God.

The life history of the Indian saints of pre-Buddhistic period is shrouded in mystery and what little we can gather of their doings is not adequate enough to present their faithful biographies. The following SHLOKA enumerates the names of these BHAKTAS:

प्रह्लाद नारद पराशर पुण्डतीक । व्यासम्बरीष शुक शौनक भीष्म दल्भियान् ।
रुक्माङ्गदार्जुन बसिष्ठ बिभीषणादीन् ॥ पुण्यान्निमान् परमभावगवतान्नमामि ॥

PRAHLADA, NARADA, VYASA, SHUKA, SHOWNAKA and Arjuna are typical examples of these saints. To these may be added the names of UDDHAVA, AKRURA, VIDURA and HANUMAN. To illustrate from the life history of each of these saints why and how these attained that eminence of saintliness lies far beyond the scope of this chapter. The PURANAS and the KAVYAS describe at great length their miracles so common to all the saints. But the greatest and the grandest of their miracles is their theism.

When we study the lives of the saints of the post-Buddhistic period we, however, run on firmer ground. Tradition and folklore afford us sufficient data to take a general survey and form an estimate of their work. Their work has left permanent footprints on the sands of time. Impact of alien systems of thought, the social cataclysms and the political changes accelerated the progress of their work. Their theism became slightly coloured by the views then current and the significance of their social and literary work became all the more greater. They became the forerunners of the great Intellectual Renaissance. Throughout the 15th, 16th and 17th centuries there was a remarkable and continued succession of these masterminds singing their songs of devotion and rousing civic consciousness of the masses throughout the country. Each province had its own saints. JNANA-SAMBHAND-HARA, TIRUVALLUVAR and TAYUMANWVAR of the Tamil country, VEMANNA of the Telugu distircts, RAMADASA and TUKARAM of the Maratha country, CHAITANYA of Bengal, KABIR and TULSIDASA of United Provinces and NANAK of the Panjab, RAMAVALLABHA DASA and APPAYA of the Kanarese Districts, delivered their messages of BHAKTI and threw open 'the gates of heaven' from the highest to the humblest. From Ramananda of the 15th century down to Ramakrishna Paramahamas of the 19th century, these saints became the originators of great spiritual and intellecual movements.

Before we refer to the different aspects of their theism, it is better we meditate on the significance of some other aspects of their work. Their work was primarily religious but it paved the way for reforms in other directions as well. In the first place, wherever they used to go and preach, they would speak in the common vernaculars of the districts. Their songs were uniformly in the language of the people. So even the common people, who had not the benefit of the study of the classical language which became practically the monopoly of a few privileged classes, could understand and appreciate the significance of their preachings. Even to this day the vernaculars of India have their literatures enriched by their songs sung in such exquisite language The Hindi language without the songs of TULASI DASA and MARATHI without the ABHANGS of JNANADEVA and TUKARAM would be nowhere. So, enrichment of the vernacular is one of the greatest of the achievements of these saints. Secondly, these devotees were great social reformers. India has been a land of castes and creeds. The caste system was originally based on the principle of division of labour. It determined an individual's position in society and was an important factor in the elimination of strife and competition from society. But in medieval India some of the worst features of this institution asserted themselves and held the society in its fatal grasp. Superciliousness of one caste for another and notions of 'touch' and 'no-touch' were eating into the vitals of the society. It was then these medieval saints stood up as the great opponents of the evil effects of caste. They freely mixed themselves with the lower castes and at times did not hesitate to abolish the restrictions imposed upon them by convention, even though they happened to be born as BRAHMANS. These saints were drawn from among the lowest of the low. Namadeva of Maharashtra was a tailor while Tukarama was a Shudra. Kabir of Northern India was a weaver while Tiruvallur of Southern India was a pariah. Tulsidasa is said to have invited a low caste deserving beggar and heedless of the protests of his people partook of his meal in his company freely. Because he knew devotion observes no caste and God makes no difference between one child of His and another. They not only worked for union and tolerance between the different sects but stood up as the great supporters of universal brotherhood.

But the bedrock of their greatness is their theism, pure and simple. Their religion consisted in a deep and emotional realisation of a Personal God. For this realisation they followed the path of NAVA VIDHA BHAKTI—Nine-fold path of devotion. The salient features of this well-known nine-fold path are clearly set forth in the following remarkable SHLOKA.

श्रवणं कीर्तनं विष्णो: स्मरणं पादसेवनम् ।
अर्चनं वन्दनं दास्यं सख्यं आत्मनिवेदनम् ॥ (Bhagavata)

The essentials are:–

1. Hearing of the great qualities of God—as illustrated in the life of SHRIKANTA.
2. Chanting the hymns in praise of God—as did PARIKSHITI.
3. Contemplation of God—as done by Prahladha.
4. Humble service rendered to God by Vaiyasaki.
5. Worship of God as was done by PRAHALADA.
6. Salutation as was done by AKRURA.
7. Disinterested service as rendered by Hanuman.
8. Seeking the friendship of God as was done by Arjuna.

and

9. Self-introspection and surrender to His will, as was illustrated in the life of BALI.

Strictly speaking, these are the different aspects of one and the same Bhakti. Says saint Rama Vallabha-dasa of Kanara:–

जैसी नवखंडीं एकाक्षिति । कीं नवत्री एकाचि कांति ॥ तैसी नवरात्री नवभक्ति ॥ भुक्ति मुक्ति एकचि ॥ ... तेंचि नव विधिहि एक भक्ति ॥

Just as the lustre found in nine jewels is the same, so also is this NAVAVIDHA-BHAKTI one. At a certain stage of the evolution of Bhakti one and all the methods merge into one great cause when the devotee realises the SAT-CHIT-ANANDA—the Supreme Bliss in himself. To reach the last rung of the ladder the following steps should be consistently and perseveringly crossed over (1) Humility (2) Earnestness (3) Faith and (4) Renunciation. Faith is essential. So also is VAIRAGYA without which the fruits of BHAKTI cannot be enjoyed. The roots of BHAKTI go deep into mysticism. Faith is the root, knowledge the branch and the Bhakti the fruit thereof.

God in Man

The saints found God not outside them but in the innermost corner of their own hearts. They never thought that pilgrimages, penances, privations and other sufferings unnecessarily inflicted on the human body were the essentials of religion. Purity of heart and sincere love to God were the essentials of Bhakti. Says Ramavallabhadasa:

माझें येथेंचि पंढरपूर ।। माझें येथेंचि पंढरपूर ।। आहां जाणें नलगें दूर ।।
अणुरेणु व्यापूनि भरोनि असतां कसें म्हणावें दूर ।। माझें ...

'My Pandharpur—place of pilgrimage—is here only. How can we say that God is there when he fills the entire universe?'

A similar question was asked by Narada to Lord Krishna. 'Where do you live?' The answer is significant:

नाहं वसामि बैकुण्ठे योगिनां हृदये रचौ ।। मद्भक्ता यत्र गायन्ति तत्र
तिष्ठामि नारद ।।

'I do not reside in Heaven, nor do I live in the hearts of YOGINS. I stay wherever my BHAKTAS sing the Glory.'

Such sentiments are embodied in the works of many saints who are all unanimous in holding that God is in man.

No Mediator

Another noteworthy feature of their theism is that, for the attainment of God, no mediator is needed. Straight could they approach him. Arjuna in all humility and sincerity of purpose asks Shri Krishna the momentous question 'How to attain Thee?' Lord answers: 'I am not to be acquired by the study of the Vedas, nor even by penance, charity or sacrifices. By disinterested piety alone you can attain Me.' That is the quintessence of BHAKTI-YOGA so vividly described in the BHAGAVADGITA. Of course many saints did seek the help of their GURUS but it was only for receiving the Light. Having once obtained the clue, they were free to chose Him in their own heart. The outpourings of the heart with the simplicity of a child do receive attention from On High. 'Give me the simplicity of a child and grant me the only boon that I may not forget Thee,' so prays Tukaram.

Purity of Heart

It is said of a saint's disciple that he wanted to go on a pilgrimage for purifying his soul. Straightaway he went to the saint and said, 'Bhagvan, I am to go to Benares to wash away my sins after a bath in the Ganges. Pray accompany me.' 'Nay,' replied the saint, 'Take this gourd on my behalf and get it washed.' The disciple took the gourd, dipped it in the Ganges river and brought it back to the GURU. 'Here, Sir, have I brought the gourd back?' 'Break it and see if its inside bitterness is gone' said the saint. 'No,' replied the disciple. 'It is as bitter as it was before.' 'Yes,' said the saint 'If the Ganges water was powerless to remove its bitterness, how can man's sins be washed and hearts be made purer? Be pure in mind and heart and sins will be washed. External bath is inefficacious for effecting internal purity.' The simple story sums up their theism. Purity of heart more than anything else is essential. 'Pure thoughts, pure words and pure deeds' are the necessary virtues to be cultivated by men in general.

Self Surrender

The devotee in all humility lays his heart open, confesses his sins, expresses his determination to love Him and seeks His mercy; करिसी तूं करि मज अपिंका देह तुज ॥ तुज वांचोनि दुजे न दिसें रे व्यापका ॥

Ramavallabhadasa: 'Do whatsover you like with me. I have surrendered this body to Thee.' Such outpourings as these raised the saints above the sensuous plane.

Introspection

Antar-dhyana, self-analysis, self-criticism, looking inwards as did the great saint Janaka of yore is the keynote of their theism. Train the mind for non-attachment, discipline the heart to look upon 'pleasure and pain' alike, attain (समाचित्तत्व) balance of mind. By constant practice and Vairagya shall thou attain Him, अभ्यास वैरागयाभ्यां तन्निरोध:. One of the most difficult paths to be trodden to be sure. But the ideal is indeed praiseworthy.

Monotheism

Relentless critics there are who hold that the theism of saints is no more than a mere crude form of the worship of stocks and stones, rocks and rivers, fields and forests. Nothing can be further from truth. There can be no denying the fact that the worship of a Personal God is traceable in their theism but diving below the surface one sees distinct traces of the existence of monotheism pure and simple. A careful reader of the works of saints like Kabir, Chaitanya, Ramadasa or even Tukaram will find that all of them did view their one Deity as the Supreme Soul pervading throughout the universe and even beyond. One without a second, call Him by any name but He is One, is what they held. As a typical example we quote only one Abhang of saint Rama-vallabha.

Lord is One. God is one. Some call Him Ganesh, some the Sun but all are ignorant. He is one.

There are positive evidences in the works of all these saints to show that they were all monotheists in reality.

It is this belief in God's omnipotence and omnipresence that made these saints work for the uplift of their fellowmen. When they found that the common people were denied the blessings of a higher spiritual life they carried the torch of light in the dark corners and roused the masses in general. Individual advance was not the goal of their ambition. They wanted their fellowmen too to realise the blessings of BHAKTI. Side by side with quiet meditation on the eternal verities they made others' lives grander and beliefs loftier. When God-consciousness is roused and man experiences the reality of his religious nature, fellowship with God and man becomes by far easier. To that end saints in India lived and died. Even in modern times men there are who have imbibed their spirit and by their motto of 'plain-living and high-thinking' have made the lives of others nobler and sublimer. Who has not lived in SHANTINIKETAN and not breathed the saintly atmosphere? Who has not paid a visit to the KANGRI GURUKUL and not felt that the institution stands a monument to the philanthrophy of a SADHU? Who can say that the women's university at Poona is not the product of the humility and disinterestedness of a modern saint? Saints lived not only in prehistoric times and medieval periods of Indian history but they are living also, even now. In recent years many of them have joined the majority but by God's grace their continuity seems not to have broken. From Ramakrishna Paramhamsa down to Ramakrishna Bhandarkar many sages have lived and are still living. Each one, great in his own field has achieved, some noble object or at least has struggled to live upto a certain ideal, whether political, social or religious. If such greatness is the outcome of the high ideals set up by the science of ethics and if in the process of nation-building each has contributed his mite, none need despair of the race and its future. There is no royal road to progress of any kind whether spiritual or temporal. Disastrous defeats, tremendous opposition and heart-rending reverses fall to the lot of every reformer in any department of human activity. Real greatness lies in overcoming all these obstructions in the path of progress. So also genuine goodness consists in patiently waiting, meekly seeking and nobly marching on to the goal, set up by the ethicists of all ages and climes, including these never-to-be forgotten worthies of India who go by the name of saints.